Greenwich Meridian Trail

Book 4: Boston to Sand le Mere

98 kilometres – 61 miles

and the
Humber Link

Cleethorpes to Patrington by Bus or Boat

Graham and Hilda Heap

*Beware the two hundred yards off the village street.
'Tis the dog bog zone, so mind your feet.*

Published by New Generation Publishing in 2016

Copyright © Graham and Hilda Heap 2016

The author asserts the moral right under the Copyright, Designs and Patents Act 1988 to be identified as the author of this work.

All Rights reserved. No part of this publication may be reproduced, stored in a retrieval system or transmitted, in any form or by any means without the prior consent of the author, nor be otherwise circulated in any form of binding or cover other than that which it is published and without a similar condition being imposed on the subsequent purchaser.

ISBN13: 978-1-78719-231-7

Cover design by Jacqueline Abromeit
Cover Image Maud Foster Windmill Boston

This product includes mapping reproduced by permission of Ordnance Survey on behalf of HMSO. © Crown copyright 2012. All rights reserved.
Ordnance Survey Licence number 100049353.

www.newgeneration-publishing.com

The Parish Church of St Patrick Patrington

Introduction

When Hilda suggested that there really ought to be a long-distance walk along the Greenwich Meridian, we both thought that such a walk just had to be devised, and wondered why it had not already been done. Now it *has* been done and we believe that it has turned out well. The route goes through a great variety of towns, villages and countryside, each part of the walk having its own quite distinctive character. In Book 1 there are the South and North Downs, the High and Low Weald and the outskirts and centre of London, each contrasting with the others. Book 2 has a different London experience; Epping Forest and the Lee Valley, both green escapes from the surrounding urban encroachment, and the very gentle Hertfordshire hills, pretty and unspoilt. Book 3 crosses the Fens, flat and spacious. Towns and villages are probably no further apart compared to many other parts of the country, but walking between them emphasises their separation, even though walking on the flat takes no effort at all.

Now we come to the final part of the walk which crosses a part of England that, while not exactly 'off the beaten track', is quite often not on the road to anywhere either. One has to have a reason for venturing into this part of the country, in our case it was the Greenwich Meridian, and what we found was both interesting and really very enjoyable. There is the opportunity to view a Lancaster bomber at East Kirkby, the ruins of the castle where King Henry IV was born and the sublime beauty of the Lincolnshire Wolds, its attraction for walkers is only increased by its relative isolation. Louth is very conscious of its position on the prime meridian, having almost as many Meridian markers as East Grinstead. It is another town stuffed full of history, and can boast of having the highest spire of any parish church in the country. Some might think that the Humber Estuary is an inconvenient impediment in the way of the trail, we see it more as an opportunity for some creative 'walking'. No other long-distance walk, as far as we know, has the possibility of a boat ride as part of the experience, though at the time of writing, details have yet to be finalised. The final few miles begin close to the parish church of St Patrick in Patrington, which is considered to be one of the most beautiful village churches in England. If you have managed to resist visiting all the other churches you have passed on this trail, relent and take some time to visit this one; it is, somehow, really quite special. The end of the walk is strangely satisfying. This windswept coastline is the fastest eroding coast in England, managing to lose, on average, about 1 metre a year. There used to be a coastal path, but that is now many, many metres out to sea. East Yorkshire County Council is building another defensive embankment which will work for a while, but the evidence of the sea's remorseless progress is clear to see. Roads end precipitously, drain pipes stick out pathetically from the soft clay 'cliffs' and the beach is strewn with huge concrete blocks from defensive structures built to repel the sea and other potential invaders, but now stranded and useless. There is a bleak beauty which is just a little disconcerting. This is man against nature and man is not winning.

One of the aims of our walk was to explore the towns, villages and countryside linked by the Greenwich Meridian and to discover some of the history of these places. We found out far more fascinating information than could ever be contained in the guidebook. For the most part we have included the most interesting and the most quirky, and some of the serendipitous connections between places on the Meridian. Let one example suffice for the moment. Boston, we discovered, is the birthplace, in 1516, of John Foxe, the martyrologist. The complete title of Foxe's *Book of Martyrs*, first published in 1563, runs to 46 words, which is one of the longest book titles known and why it is usually known, simply, as Foxe's *Book of Martyrs*. In it, he gives an account of Christian martyrs from the 1st to the 16th century AD. However, it was the strong emphasis on the suffering of Protestants, particularly during the reign of Queen Mary, that stoked the fires of anti-Catholicism and this has resonated down the centuries. We first met that at Lewes, with its strongly anti-popery bonfire societies of the past; then there is the memorial to Protestant martyrs in Stratford and finally, we discovered the failed Rye House Plot, in 1683, to assassinate King Charles II and his brother James, which was an attempt to prevent James, a Catholic, succeeding to the throne.

We wanted to create an interesting, challenging and memorable walk using public rights of way as close to the Meridian as possible. Most of the time we have managed to stay quite remarkably close and the paths have linked together relatively easily, but there have also been many places where we have had to make difficult choices. Usually we have chosen footpaths that are away from the Meridian instead of a closer road, but in some places road walking is the only real option. Sometimes, we had to choose between two equally attractive or interesting routes. We think we have got the balance as right as it is ever likely to be.

Acknowledgements

Many people have helped during the course of planning and walking the trail and the production of this guidebook. In no particular order we should like to thank – Andrew Chudley, Jonathan Stockdale, Martin and Bev Gosling, Ralph Ward, Jan Crowther, Malcolm McBeath, Rachel Shaw, James Forester, Susan Archibald, John Sparshatt, Paul Lawrence and Charles Sutcliffe.

Thanks also to – Martin and Bev Gosling, Rachel Shaw, Andrew Panton, John Large, Susan Archibald, Catrina Appleby, Becky Wallower, Peter Burley, David Plant, Kevin Crowe, Steven Lumb, David Edgar and Graham Matthews for allowing us to use information from their publications and websites.

Our thanks also go to everybody at IndePenPress and especially to Kathryn and Catriona whose expertise and patience have made these guidebooks look as good as they do.

Our special thanks go to Graham King who has willingly led some members of our walking group along the trail using our directions, without the benefit of a map, and in so doing has highlighted many deficiencies which we have been able to correct. Also to Ann and Bill Wheaton who, at the beginning of this project, followed our route for the entire length of the trail, gave us invaluable feedback, suggested improvements to the route, and it was their enthusiasm for the idea that kept us going when our enthusiasm threatened to wane.

Using the Guidebook

The description of the route is clear and comprehensive. Each section is coordinated with the adjacent map and the book will fit into most map holders. The route has been checked against locally held definitive maps. Where we have used permissive paths, we have ensured that an alternative route is mentioned should the permissive path be closed. If you have any problems, please get in touch with the publishers.

The snippets of information within the guide were gleaned from many sources. Bing was much used. Local authority and local community websites and Wikipedia were all helpful. Pevsner proved useful on occasions. Sources are given at the end of the guide.

For small villages the facilities are given in some detail, but for large villages and towns details are limited to accommodation and transport as all the usual shops will be found.

The walk has been broken up into sections that coincide with convenient towns. Accommodation is plentiful, less so in The Fens, and more or less in the right places. Tourist Information Centres will be able to furnish you with an up-to-date list, or email the authors at hilda_heap@btinternet.com

There are plenty of places to jump on and off buses and trains, making it easy to walk short sections at a time. Online travel information sites are very good. The section on public transport gives distances from the start of each section in order to facilitate planning your walk.

Introduction to the Second Edition

We have walked this part of the trail, one way or another, five times, the last time in order to update the directions for this new edition of the guide. We continue to be enthralled by the lovely countryside, the impressive coastline and the many towns and villages with their interesting buildings and histories. Knowing virtually nothing about this part of England before we started this venture, we are more than happy that by dint of the Greenwich Meridian passing through it we have discovered all the attractions to be found along the route of this part of the trail.

Distance checklist

This list will assist you in calculating the distance between places on the trail where you may be planning to stay overnight or to access public transport.

	Distance between Locations		**Cumulative Distance**	
Location	km	miles	km	miles
Boston to Stickford+ (1)	19.5	12	19.5	12
Stickford to Tetford*	20	12.5	39.5	24.5
Tetford to Louth*	15.5	9.5	55	34
Louth to Cleethorpes (Meridian)*	28	17.5	83	51.5
Patrington to Hollym*	5.5	3.5	88.5	55
Hollym to Sand le Mere	9.5	6	98	61
Sand le Mere to Withernsea*	4.5	3		

Key:

* = accommodation and public transport
+ = public transport only
(1) Catch a bus here for accommodation at West Keale and Spilsby

The Route in Sections

Patrington to Sand le Mere
15km - 9.5 miles

Sand le Mere

Patrington

The Humber Link by
bus or boat

Cleethorpes

Louth to Cleethorpes
28km - 17.5 miles

Louth

Tetford

Boston to Louth
55km - 34 miles

Hagworthingham

Stickford

Boston

Boston to Louth

55 kilometres – 34 miles

At first we are still in Fen country and soon the discipline of straight roads by straight drains sets in, with some welcome variation around Sibsey and Stickney. Slowly getting closer are the undulating hills of the Lincolnshire Wolds, rightly designated as an area of outstanding natural beauty. There is something comely about its gentle hills, quietly decorous, nothing flashy, simply pleasing and rather a nice change from the Fens.

OS Maps:
Explorer 261: Boston
Explorer 273: Lincolnshire Wolds South
Explorer 282: Lincolnshire Wolds North.

Boston

Boston can be traced back to 645AD when Botolph established a monastery on the banks of the River Witham. The parish church, dedicated to St Botolph, is one of the largest in England and its beautiful and impressive tower, at 272 feet (83m), the highest of any parish church, dominates the town. Affectionately known as the 'Boston Stump', probably because of its appearance from the surrounding countryside, it was used by bomber pilots as a landmark when returning home in WWII. Pevsner describes the church, started in 1309, as a "giant amongst English parish churches" but is less impressed with the height of the tower, which he puts down to the "hubris" which "gripped the Bostonians" in the late middle ages when building an "exceedingly high tower was a universal ambition" not only in this country but also on the continent.

Boston's past prosperity is reflected in the wealth of historic buildings. The Guildhall dates from 1390 and has many original features remaining. Next door is Fydell House which dates from 1726 and has a mulberry tree in the garden. It contains the 'American Room' which was opened by the US Ambassador, Joseph Kennedy, in 1938. The Maud Foster windmill was built in 1819 for Thomas and Isaac Reckitt. They sold it in 1833, and after a chequered history the windmill itself became unusable in 1948. Mr Basil Reckitt, great-grandson of Isaac Reckitt, ensured its survival with essential repairs in 1953, but its present state, in full, glorious working order is down to the dedication and hard work of the Waterfield family who acquired the mill in 1987. Visiting days are Wednesday and Saturday. The mill is named after the adjacent drain. It was cut in 1568 through land owned by Maud Foster, a wealthy local-landowner. The Stump and Candle Public House stands on the site of the birthplace of John Foxe, previously mentioned in the introduction. His *Book of Martyrs* turned him into a celebrity overnight and was second only to the Bible in terms of numbers sold. Foxe was possibly the first author to try to corroborate the information given to him about martyrs and to include these sources of information for the reader. He was, perhaps, the first modern historian.

Getting to the start

From the railway station, go ahead down Station Street and into Lincoln Lane. Bear right through police station car park then left through small 'park' and cross the river into Market Place.

From Market Place, with St. Botolphs on your left, go ahead into Strait Bargate. Carry on into Wide Bargate, walking up the left-hand pavement, passing the post office and war memorial. At Boston Shopping Park, turn right over traffic lights, go ahead on A16 towards Grimsby, cross Maud Foster Drain and turn left up Willoughby Road. Keep on this for almost 2km, soon passing the splendid windmill. After crossing railway keep ahead along straight bridleway through gate. At the end follow bridleway to right of house, turn left along footpath, cross drain near Cowbridge House Inn and turn right onto road. Walk up for 100m, turn right along footpath over sluice, go ahead across golf course fairway, then turn left and walk along side of course with water on your right. At bridges go ahead then follow path left to come out into golf club car park.

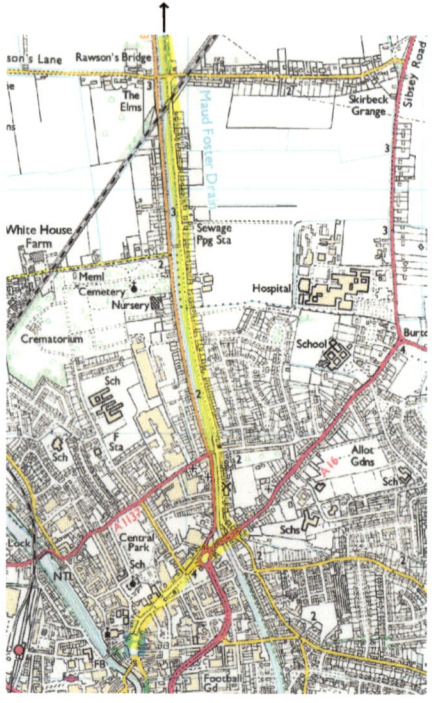

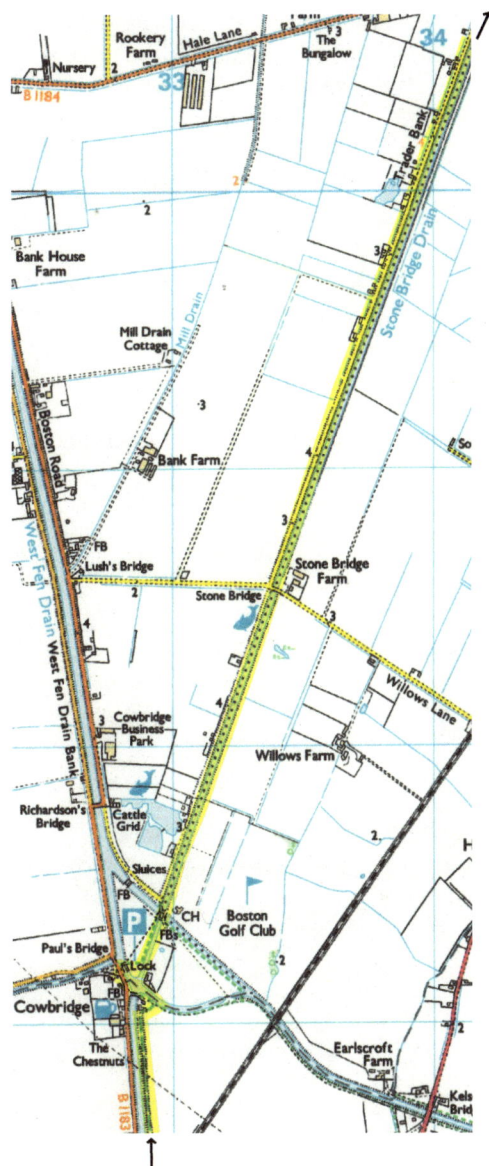

Keep ahead on track, with practice area on left and Stone Bridge Drain on right. Follow the track, which is managed by the Environment Agency and open to the public as a footpath, for 1km and at road go ahead with water still on your right for about 2.5km.

At junction, turn right over bridge, walk along for 200m then turn left up path towards Sibsey Trader Windmill. Built in 1877 and now restored, this six storey mill is opened by English Heritage most weekends and has a country tearoom to tempt you to stop awhile. There is a pub and a shop with post office in Sibsey village.

Follow path to right of outbuildings and keep ahead across field to bridge. Keep on across next field, go through gap and keep ahead. Cross ditch and follow the path diagonally right, across field. Cross bridge and stay on same heading. At the end of hedgerow follow path left, walk along with hedgerow on left, cross ditch and carry on along left edge of field. Cross stile, keep ahead, cross second stile and go across field towards houses ahead. At road, go ahead up Goosemuck Lane and at the end, follow path along edge of field, with hedge on your left.

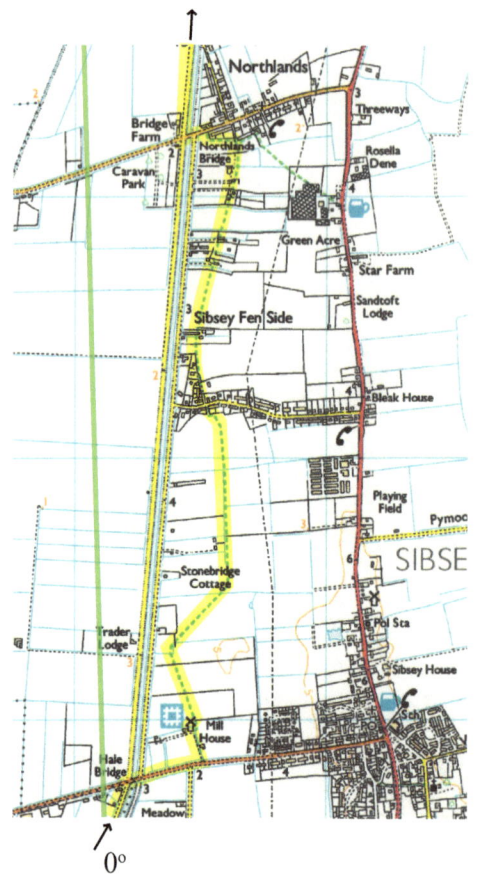

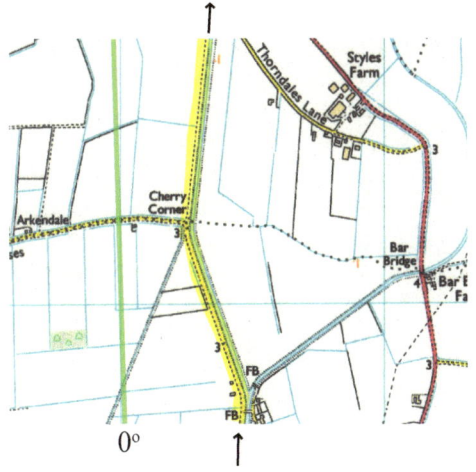

At field edge go left, then right over stile and footbridge, through garden, over stile and keep ahead across grassed drive belonging to house on your right. Cross footbridge into field, follow path ahead through a succession of stiles, bridges, driveways and gardens for the next 1km till you reach Northlands where, with back gardens ahead, you turn left and at end of houses turn right onto road. Turn left, walk along road for 200m, cross drain, turn immediately right and follow road with drain on your right for 1km. At Cherry Corner, where road goes left, go through gap ahead and then bear right onto path on top of the bank with hedge on your left. (This path is not a right of way, but is well used by the locals. Both the Environment Agency and the owners are happy for it to be used as a footpath).

Sibsey Trader Windmill

Keep on path for 1km and at Grange Bridge, turn right over drain then find footpath over footbridge on your left, turn right across field to stile to the right of house, cross drive and second stile into field. Go diagonally left to find footbridge at the right end of nearest hedgerow, cross tracks and keep ahead with hedge on your right through field used for car boot sales. At corner of field, go through gap, keep ahead across field and then with ditch on right. Cross footbridge, bear slightly right to keep along in same general direction. Cross ditch and stiles, keep ahead to stile on right of farm buildings and walk through to road.

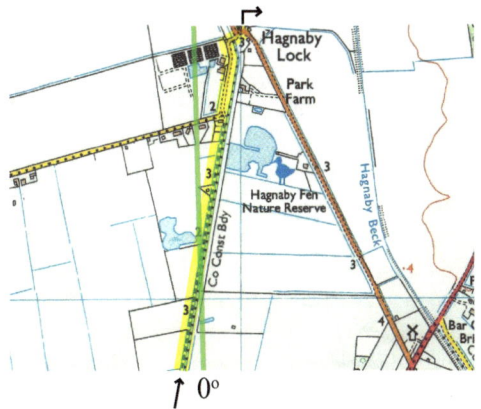

↑ 0°

Stickney
The village has a very good history website. Here you can find out about the development of the Alford to Boston turnpike and the history of the local bank, but more intriguing is the entertaining account of the time Paul Verlaine, the French poet, spent in Stickney as a schoolmaster. Most of his life was one of drink, drugs and debauchery but for the year 1875 to 76 that he spent in Stickney, his behaviour was described as exemplary and he was well liked by his pupils at William Lovell's School, not least for his brilliant caricatures of himself and some of the local notables. His time in Stickney was an attempt by Verlaine to reform his life after he had been imprisoned for 18 months for shooting his lover, the teenage poet Arthur Rimbaud, in the arm in a drunken jealous rage. Rimbaud survived. Verlaine was a much-admired major poet of the Symbolist movement. He was elected France's Prince of Poets by his peers, but died in poverty soon after in 1896, aged 51, from drinking too much absinthe in Parisian cafés.

Facilities: public house with food; village store; post office; telephone; doctor; buses.

Turn left, cross Meridian, walk along for 400m, cross drain, and turn right up footpath which follows track to Bank Farm with drain on right. At farm keep ahead along enclosed path and keep on beside drain for the next 3km. At houses, keep ahead up road and follow it right over bridge.

Lancaster Bomber Just Jane

Go ahead at junction and turn right along footpath behind the Jolly Sailor Inn (now a private house). Follow path along edge of field with ditch on your right and after about 300m follow path as it goes left then right to find footbridge (beside trees) across stream. Go ahead across field towards buildings and walk out to the road. Turn left and follow this road for 1km. The Wolds are getting ever closer. At junction turn left, and keep on for the next 2km, passing the end of the disused landing strip on your right. At crossroads with the A155 in Hagnaby go ahead and walk up to Old Bolingbroke. About 200m after entering village turn right along footpath towards village centre. At end of path, cross stream and keep ahead onto road. Follow road left then turn left after 150m, along road that is 'unsuitable for coaches and heavy goods vehicles' and walk up past castle entrance to church and The Black Horse public house.

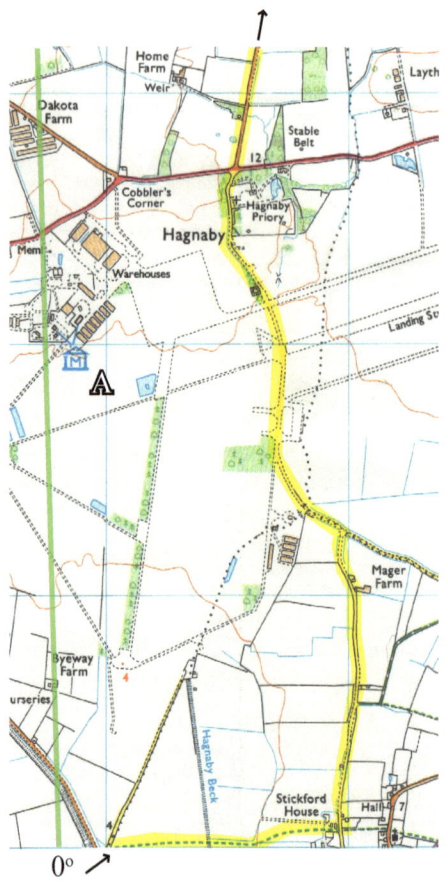

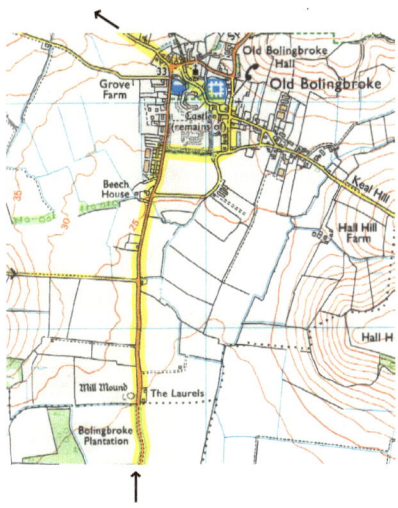

Lincolnshire Aviation Heritage Centre in East Kirkby (A)

The entrance is almost 1km from Hagnaby crossroads. Opened in 1988 by two farming brothers, Fred and Harold Panton, this privately-owned and run museum is a tribute to their oldest brother Christopher, who was killed on a bombing raid over Nuremburg in March 1944, and a memorial to the 55,573 men of Bomber Command who lost their lives during WWII. Before the building of the National Memorial in Green Park in London, inaugurated in June 2012, and the placing of a memorial on Beachy Head in the same year, this Heritage Centre was the only memorial to all those brave men. The collection on show is evocative and moving. For not an inconsiderable amount of money you can taxi around the airfield in Just Jane, a real, noisy Lancaster bomber. Refreshments are served in the well-run 'NAAFI' café. The fact that the Greenwich Meridian runs through the middle is an entirely trivial reason for making the effort to visit this important museum.

Old Bolingbroke Castle and Church

The Royal Village of Old Bolingbroke

The castle came into the possession of John of Gaunt, the third son of King Edward III, through his marriage to Blanche of Lancaster in 1359. His son, Henry Bolingbroke, later King Henry IV, was born there in 1366. John became de facto ruler of England when his elder brother, the Black Prince, died in 1376 and his father became too ill to rule. He was the richest man in England and wielded considerable power. He was able to force parliament to impose the first poll tax in English history. This and his ostentatious lifestyle, including an enormous mansion in London called the Savoy Palace, led to his increasing unpopularity in the country. During the Peasants' Revolt of 1381 (Book 1: Blackheath) the rebels utterly destroyed the Savoy Palace and would have killed John had he been in London. Fortunately for him, he was visiting Scotland and was able to take refuge with the Scottish King Robert II until the rebellion was crushed.

His nephew, the 14-year-old King Richard II, showed enormous courage when he faced down the rebel army with the cry of "You shall have no captain but me." However, he grew up to be a divisive king obsessed with his belief that he had been divinely appointed as king and, as such, could rule as he pleased without consulting parliament or the great barons, in this way breaking his coronation oath to rule justly and for the good of the people. In 1387, his powers had been curtailed by a group of earls calling themselves the 'Lords Appellant', against whom he took revenge in 1397. Two were killed and one banished. John of Gaunt, up to then a powerful ally and stabilising influence, was old and ill. Unrestrained, Richard began again to act out his delusions of divine power. Having banished Bolingbroke for reasons too involved to go into here, the king then seized the vast estates of John of Gaunt, after Gaunt's death, denying Bolingbroke his rightful inheritance. Such hubris alienated parliament and the barons, who feared for their own positions. When Henry returned from exile and forced Richard to surrender, parliament was easily persuaded to depose Richard, declaring him a tyrant, and acclaim Henry as King, though, according to Simon Sharma, not loudly enough, and Henry himself asked for another, more heartfelt, expression of support. Henry's coronation followed quickly. He was the first monarch to address his people in English and he had the support of parliament, but his reign was riven by dissent. His grounds for claiming the crown were entirely spurious and many in the country would not accept his usurping of the throne. By this act he set in train the events that were eventually played out in the War of the Roses, some 50 years later.

The castle remained a royal residence, though Henry never visited after he became king. After the Tudor period, it gradually fell into decay, but its present ruinous state dates from the Civil War. A Royalist stronghold, it held out against parliamentary forces, expecting relief from an approaching Royalist army. This, however, was routed at the nearby Battle of Winceby in 1643 and the garrison was forced to surrender. After the war ended the castle was demolished, much of the stone being reused locally. As far as we know, this is the only royal village in the country.

Facilities: public house with food; post box; telephone; buses (must be booked at least 2 hours in advance on 0845 234 3344).

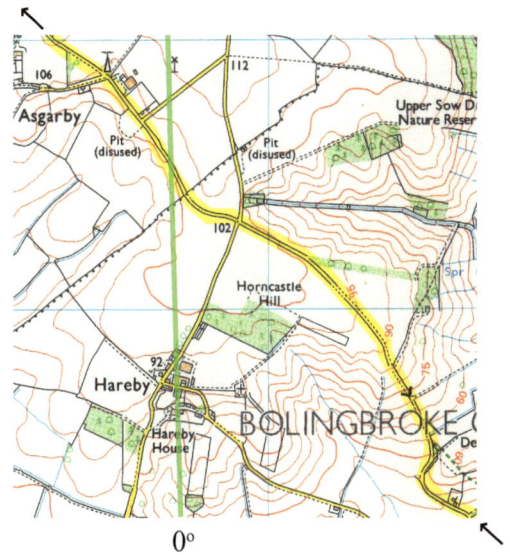

Cross over to the right of the war memorial and leave the village on the road to Asgarby and Horncastle. Follow this road for nearly 2km as it climbs up into the charming scenery of the Lincolnshire Wolds. At crossroads keep ahead, following sign to Asgarby, and stay on the road for the next 2.5km to Winceby, enjoying the views looking south.

Battle of Winceby 1643
With only around 3000 troops on each side and lasting no more than half an hour, this was a minor battle in the English Civil War, but its significance is greater than the scale of the encounter. The army was commanded by the Earl of Manchester but it was the parliamentary cavalry led by Oliver Cromwell which, with the first charge, began the rout of the royalist cavalry. This was completed by a devastating flank attack by Sir Thomas Fairfax. Cromwell's horse was killed under him and he was wounded, but he managed to find another horse, remount and fight on. This defeat by Cromwell's well-equipped and well-trained cavalry, later called 'Ironsides' by Prince Rupert signalled the end of the dominance of the royalist cavalry. Parliamentary troops pursued the fleeing royalists all the way to Horncastle, killing many and taking some 800 prisoners. In all, around 300 royalist troops were killed compared to 20 or so parliamentarians. Fairfax, with Cromwell, created the New Model Army which finally destroyed the royalist cause in 1645-6.

At the junction with the B1195, keep ahead towards the house in the trees, cross road and go over stile. Bear right to cross field diagonally towards trees and find stile into Snipe Dales Nature Reserve (not quite as shown on the OS map).

Snipe Dales Country Park and Nature Reserve
The trees of the country park were planted in 1965 with pines, beech and other deciduous trees. The pines are now being replaced by native, broad-leaved trees. The separate nature reserve is one of few semi-natural wet valley systems still surviving, with two main valleys fretted by streams. It is more open than the country park. The diversity of habitats in the two areas supports a wide range of birds and other wildlife, including butterflies and dragonflies. The whole area of 90 hectares (223 acres) is jointly managed by Lincolnshire County Council and Lincolnshire Wildlife Trust.

Follow path through trees and then right along path with fence on your left. At corner of field follow path left, cross stile, go down the hill and through gate, by large gate, and stay on path to the valley floor. Cross stream, turn right and continue on path as it winds its way beside the stream, marked by square red route markers. Turn left, climb out of the valley passing through two gates and stay on broad grassy path soon with fence and then ditch on right. When you reach the finger post pointing to Hagworthingham, keep ahead following the sign to Snipe Dales Country Park.

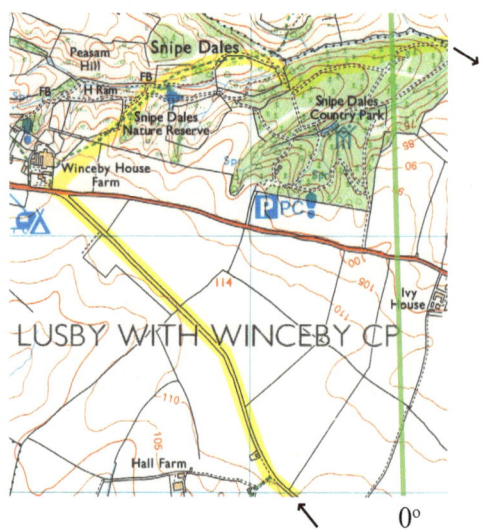

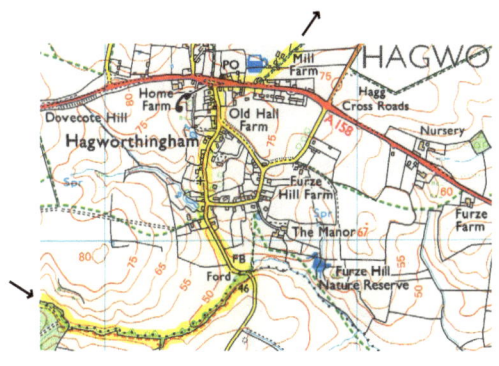

(Dog owners should go left here, staying on the public footpath, to Hagworthingham and re-join the route in the village). Drop down to valley floor, climb left then right and at the top turn left, staying with the red markers. After about 250m, where overhead power lines cross, turn left, following the red markers. Stay on the path for another 100m or so and you will come to a Meridian marker. (Turn right here and follow signs to the car park, about 800m away, where you will find toilets and information centre).

Meridian Stone
This is a neat chunk of Spilsby Sandstone. The plaque reminds us of the importance of John Harrison, who lived at Barrow-on-Humber, and his maritime chronometer with which he solved the 'longitude problem' for ships at sea. His work was finally recognised in 1773, three years before his death. His story is told by an exhibition in Flamsteed House at the Royal Observatory. We hope that you took the time to look at it when you walked through Greenwich. It really is well worth a visit.

Stay ahead with the red markers and drop down gently on the broad path. At the valley bottom follow footpath sign to Hagworthingham. Cross stream, take the path on the left of the gates and continue with fence on your right. Go through kiss gate and stay on path with fence on your right for the next 400m, with a very wiggly stream below on your left. At the road turn left, cross stream, pass a large pair of gates on your left and walk up into the village, passing church, war memorial and second-hand shop until you reach A158.

Hagworthingham

The name does not exactly 'trip off the tongue' so we are indebted to Peter Skipworth, who explains it all in the exemplary Parish Council website. In the Domesday Book it is Hacberdingham. By 1115 it had become Hagordingeheim. 'Hacberd' (becoming Hagworth) was the name of the Saxon lord and 'ing' means 'the followers of'. The'"ham' means homestead or estate so the whole name means 'the estate or homestead of the family and the people of Hacberd'. Holy Trinity Church is probably Saxon and used to have a large tower which fell down in 1972. Pevsner notes the "herringbone laying of the stones in the two middle bays of the nave N wall" which indicates an 11th century construction. The size of the tower also suggests an early date, which might be the reason why it fell down. Or it might have been the weight of the eight bells which used to hang there. The bells survived the collapse of the tower and were sold and re-hung in St Chads, the parish church of Welbourn, a village some 48km (30 miles) to the east. Once rung by eight brothers called Hubbard, D L Brown notes that there is a belief that these bells were the inspiration for Tennyson's "wild bells" in his poem *In Memoriam A.H.H.* That honour belongs to Waltham Abbey. The relevant lines were written after the Tennyson family moved to High Beach which is situated on the edge of Epping Forest some two miles from Waltham Abbey. However, the bells of Hagworthingham were almost certainly one of the "Four voices of four hamlets round - The merry, merry bells of Yule" from the same poem.

Facilities: public house with food, café; second-hand shop; post box; telephone; buses.

At the top of Church Lane, turn right and walk along on the right-hand pavement of the busy A158, towards Sausthorpe, for about 150m to the George and Dragon public house. Turn left across road and take the footpath to the right of the public house. Follow the track with farm buildings on your left and then, at house on left, keep ahead onto a grassy path. Stay on path across field, cross stile and next field then go over stile by gate onto road.

Turn left down road between trees and after 400m pass piggery on your left and follow rough track as it bends left. Stay on this bridleway, cross stream on bridge by ford and climb out of valley on stony track. After about 300m, keep ahead as stony track goes right. Follow this track between hedgerows and after 300m cross another stream at a ford. Stay on the track for about 1km as it winds its way into Bag Enderby. You are now in Tennyson country.

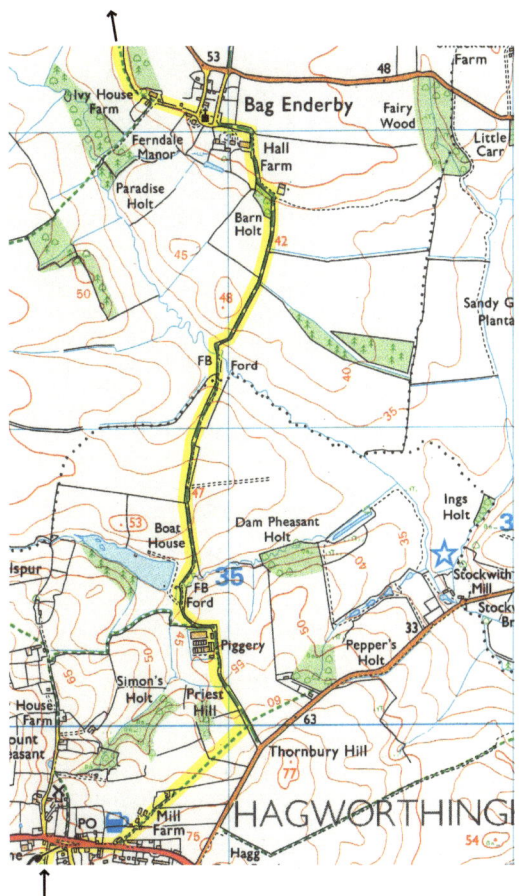

Bag Enderby

The church, dedicated to St. Margaret, dates to 1407. It is built in the Perpendicular style of greensand, the rock which underlies the chalk in these parts. The money for its construction came from the estate of Albinus de Enderby, who is commemorated on a sepulchral slab. On the door is nailed the boss of a shield of Saxon or Danish origin, depending on which source you believe. The octagonal font has some very pretty carvings and fragments of medieval glass are visible in the segmental arches of the windows. They depict the arms of Croyland Abbey, near Spalding, together with knives and scourges from the Abbey. There was a strange custom of giving little knives to anyone visiting the Abbey on St. Bartholomew's Day. How these fragments of glass came to be at Bag Enderby is not known. There used to be a very fine peal of bells which would have been another one the four Christmas Bells in Tennyson's poem, previously mentioned.

Facilities: buses (must be booked at least 2 hours in advance on 0845 234 3344).

Tennyson's Early Life

Alfred Lord Tennyson was born in 1809 in Somersby and spent the first 28 years of his life there. We are indebted to John Large for much of the information about Tennyson and the villages of Lincolnshire that follows. His publications are listed in the bibliography and available locally at Stockwith Mill and in Somersby Church. They give a vivid picture of the Tennyson family and the life and times of Lincolnshire in those days. Alfred was the fourth child of the Reverend George Clayton Tennyson and his wife Elizabeth nee Fytche, daughter of the Vicar of Louth. His upbringing, with ten siblings, was somewhat chaotic. The boys played wildly in the surrounding countryside, always looked scruffy and the family was described by the daughter of neighbouring landowner as "delightfully unconventional." Rather less charitably their cook remarked in Alfred's hearing, "If you raked out hell with a small-tooth comb, you wouldn't find their like." Alfred was tall like his father and had the reputation as the strongest boy in the village, excelling in the local sport of crowbar throwing, and once amused guests by carrying a Shetland pony around the rectory lawn. He and Charles delighted in holding the bridge over Somersby Brook against the village boys. On holiday in Skegness, then a small fishing village, the children would run wild on the beach in their bare feet from dawn to dusk.

Alfred's father, George Clayton, was ill-suited to the life of a country parson. An erudite man, he was forced to take holy orders by his father who disinherited him in favour of his younger brother, Charles. Embittered by this and his lack of preferment within the church, Alfred's father suffered bouts of depression and violent outbursts under the influence of alcohol. Nevertheless, George Clayton did manage to educate Alfred and Charles at home before they both went up to Cambridge in 1828. There Alfred met Arthur Hallam and the two became inseparable friends. Alfred was forced to leave Cambridge in 1831, when his father died, to take charge of family affairs. In 1833 Arthur Hallam died of a brain haemorrhage in Vienna. Alfred was heartbroken. All his sorrow is poured out in his poem *In Memoriam A.H.H.* finally published in 1850, the same year he was appointed Poet Laureate and married Emily Sellwood.

At the church go ahead through gap in hedge, pass church on right, leave the churchyard through the gate and go straight ahead down road opposite. After 200m, as track goes left, keep ahead down a grassy path, with a thatched cottage on your left. After about 40m, turn left onto grassy track which then bends right to run along the edge of a large field with hedgerow on your right and the buildings of Somersby seen ahead. After 200m, cross stile on your left and go diagonally across the field towards buildings seen ahead to the left. Cross two stiles and go directly ahead to house. Leave field over stile, keep ahead and then turn right through farmyard to road. Turn left and walk into the village, following signs to Greetham and Horncastle. Pass the rectory on your left and follow the road as it drops down to cross the River Lymn and then out of the valley. At the T-junction, stay ahead towards Salmonby and Tetford.

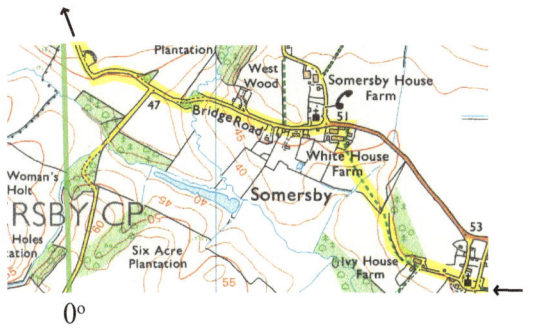

0°

Somersby

In the church is the font where Alfred Tennyson and his siblings were Christened, it is very simple, rather like the rest of the interior. Notice the groove in the column nearest the door into which a box-pew was once fitted. In the porch is a holy water stoup from the days before the Commonwealth and in the churchyard a fine Perpendicular cross which somehow survived the vandalism of Cromwell's men in the name of Puritanism. The Grange opposite, built in 1722, may well have been designed by Sir John Vanbrugh who used an almost identical design for a Nunnery at Greenwich. Next door is the Rectory where the Tennyson family lived. Alfred shared a room with a window in the gable at the top of the house. On one occasion, John Large recounts, he answered the hoot of an owl with such authenticity that the bird flew into the room.

Facilities: buses (must be booked at least 2 hours in advance on 0845 234 3344).

Somersby Church and Cross

Follow the road for 700m, passing on your right an old disused quarry with native art carved in the soft sandstone. About 200m after a sharp left hand bend turn right up bridleway along edge of field with hedge on your left and follow this for the next 600m. At corner of field go through gap, bear left along enclosed path, after 100m turn right along path between fences and walk out to road. Turn left, walk up 90m and turn right up East Road which takes you to the centre of the village.

Tetford

In the church of St Mary is a memorial to Captain Edward Dymoke, who died in 1793, the King's Champion to George II. This hereditary position began in the reign of Richard II in 1372. John Large explains all. It was the Champion's duty to ride into Westminster Hall when the banquet was taking place after the coronation service on a "good horse and well-armed for war". He would then throw down the gauntlet and challenge any person who dares "deny or gainsay Our Lord King (or Queen)" to mortal combat. King George IV put an end to this practice but the champion still has the honour of carrying the Standard of England at coronations. The Greenwich Meridian passes a few yards to the east of the church and this is marked by a modest marker beside the road. The owners of the herd of Tetford Longhorns recognise their place on the line by marketing their beef, in their shop in Louth, under the name of Meridian Meats. The longhorn is Britain's oldest beef breed and it was saved from near extinction by a small band of dedicated breeders during the 1970s. It is now off the endangered list with over 6000 registered breeding females and around 450 bulls. Although the bulls look particularly fearsome, with their bulk and long horns, in reality they are as docile as can be. If you should meet one with his heifers in a field, do not be alarmed. They may well approach out of curiosity, but will not attack.

Facilities: Accommodation – B&B and cafe at campsite; B&B, food and shop at The White Hart Inn; post box; doctors; buses.

Keep up East Road, pass church on right (turn right along road to find the Meridian Marker on the left after a few metres) and go ahead up path between houses. Pass in front of cottage on your left, go to right of garage to find bridge and stile into field. Bear right across field and cross footbridge, bear left (look out for Longhorns) then cross stile onto road. Turn left, walk up road and continue ahead up footpath to right of house. Cross stile, follow path ahead across field, go through hedgerow and climb up hill ahead on path through very large field. At the top you will enjoy nearly all round views, including the sea on the horizon to the east. Bear slightly right and cross next field.

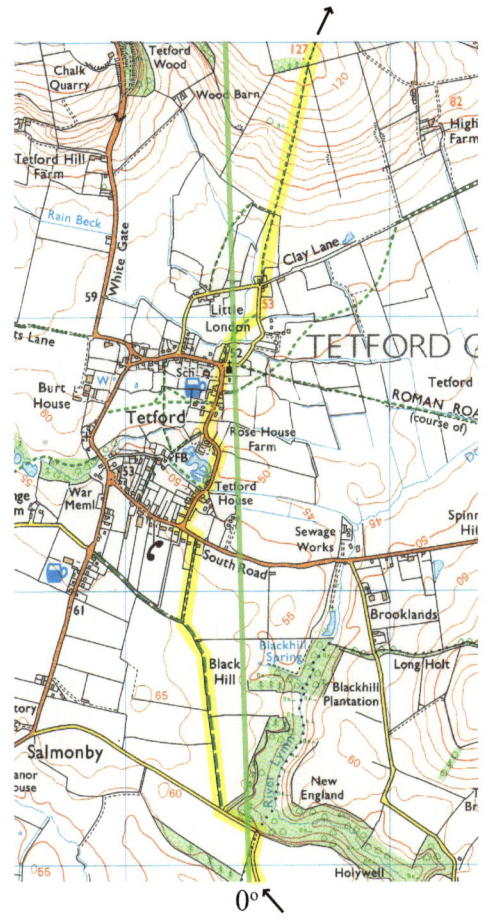

Tetford Querida, Tetford Jedi and Tetford Rowan

Go through hedge, cross corner of field and drop down onto track. Turn left, walk up 100m then follow footpath going diagonally right across field. At road turn right, walk along 80m then turn left across stile by gate. Bear right, cross field diagonally, heading to the right of the house, and find stile out of the field. Go ahead onto road and walk along with trees on your left and the wide open field on your right. Keep on the road as it curves left with farm buildings on your left. Follow road right, drop down gently into valley floor and keep on this road as it goes left and continue on for the next 1km passing between lakes and ponds. At T-junction, turn right, follow road as it drops into valley, then climb out up steep hill and where track goes off right to Ruckland church, climb up the embankment ahead on your left.

Accommodation: continue up the road for nearly 1km for the Youth Hostel at Woody's Top.

Turn left, follow path along left edge of fields for about 800m, with woods on your left. Join track coming in from your left (over stream) and bear right up track (not quite as shown on map). Follow it as it climbs and winds up the side of the valley. At Farforth Church turn right and follow road for 600m to junction. Turn right then, after 50m, turn left along straight road to Maidenwell Farm.

Maidenwell
This small hamlet was once owned by the Corporation of Basingstoke. They acquired it in 1713 from the estate of Sir James Lancaster when the trustees of the estate were unable to pay the annuities charged to the estate out of income. Sir James, a native of Basingstoke, was a great Elizabethan sailor who distinguished himself against the Spanish Armada and then went on to amass a large fortune from leading expeditions to the Far East, returning with many riches. He bought the estate at Maidenwell in 1608, possibly because the land was cheaper than agricultural land round Basingstoke, but there is no record of him having visited during the ten years before his death in 1618. Basingstoke Corporation hung onto the land for 250 years, eventually selling it in 1977. This area was once the site of the largest arable field in the country. It was known as Burwell Walk and measured over 189 acres (76 hectares).

Keep ahead through farmyard and climb right to leave yard along bridleway through trees. Follow path slightly right across a huge field (part of Burwell Walk?). The scenery now is reminiscent of the South Downs.

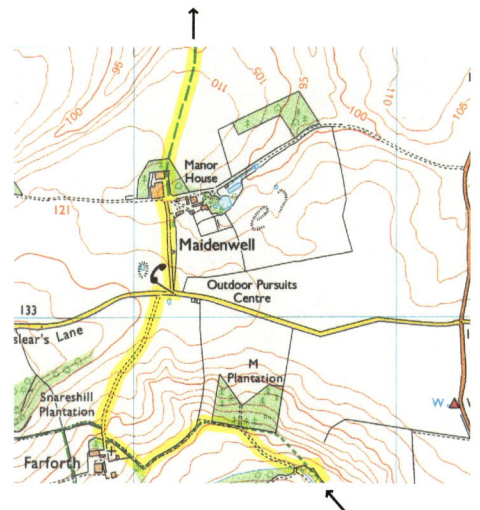

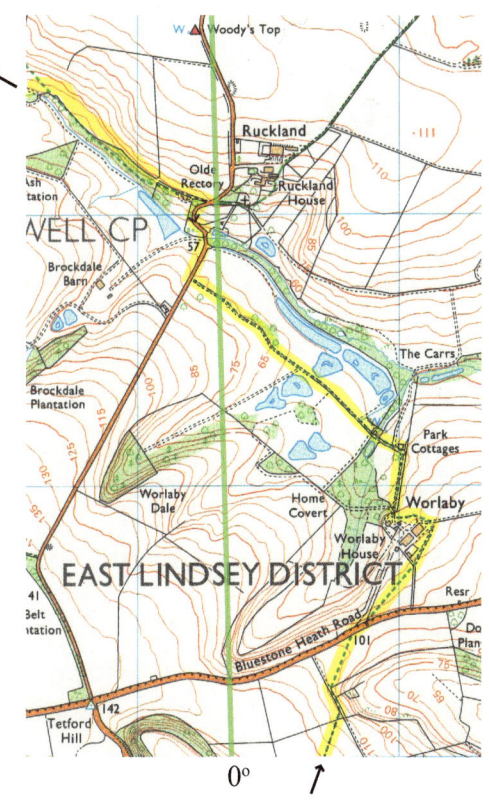

At field edge, where two tracks come in from the right, keep going ahead between more big fields. Walk up with hedge on your right and at the top, keep ahead along bridleway across field, bearing slightly right. Go through gap, keep ahead up gentle rise and follow broad grassy path with hedge on your left and the spire of Louth church seen directly ahead. Drop down to buildings, bear left onto track, keep ahead onto road and continue ahead down into village.

Tathwell

The church is dedicated to St Vedast who was Bishop of Arras in 6th century Gaul. He helped restore Christianity to that part of the country after years of destruction by invading barbarians. He is remembered for his charity, meekness and patience. Little known in England, there is only one other church dedicated to him, St Vedast alias Foster in London. Foster is the English form of Vedast by way of Vastes, Fastes, Faster, Fauster and Forster. The lower half of the tower is Norman the rest of the church is Georgian. Inside is a wall-monument to Edward Hamby, who died in 1626. It includes an image of a son who died in the same year. Pevsner quotes the entire poetic inscription, something we have not found in any other entry. One can only assume that it must have affected him quite deeply.

Facilities: post box; telephone; buses (must be booked at least 2 hours in advance on 0845 234 3344).

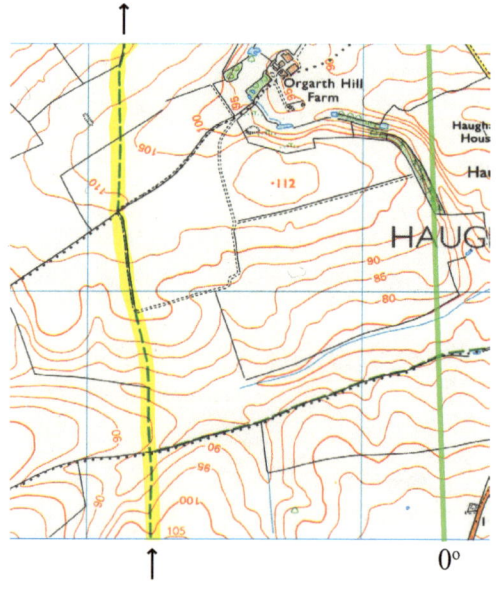

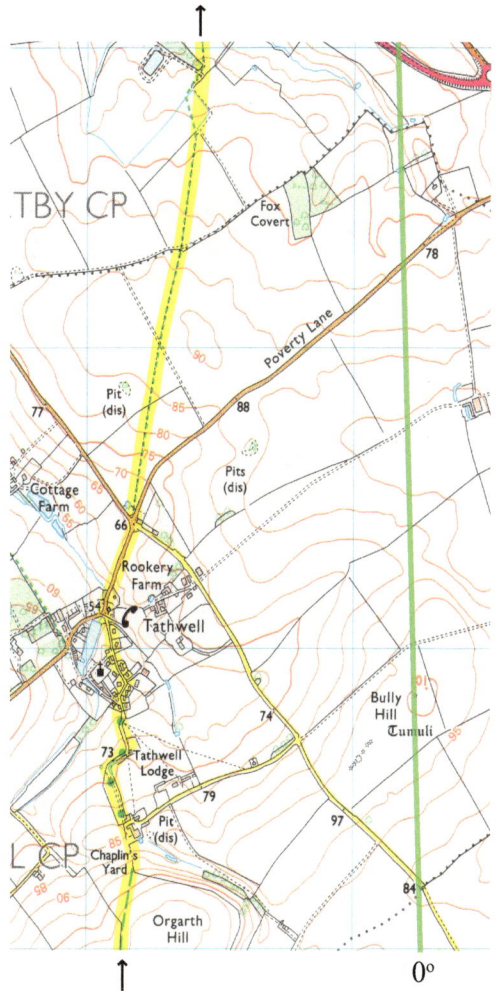

At T-junction turn right and walk up to crossroads. Take the footpath ahead on your left, go through hedgerow and climb up rise ahead along path bearing slightly left away from hedgerow on your right. Go through to next field and keep ahead in same direction. At the top the spire of Louth Church is seen ahead, cross track and follow path ahead that bears slightly right across field. Cross track and follow path towards spire. At edge of field go through hedge, cross bridge and turn right onto path along edge of field with trees on your right. After 200m, curve right onto track coming from your right. Follow this, with hedgerow on right, and at corner of next field go diagonally left across field on indistinct path, the spire just seen ahead.

Continue down the hill, cross bridge and keep ahead up path that brings you out onto busy A16. Climb up the path ahead, cross stile and bear slightly left across field (no clear path when we walked it at ploughing time) then keep ahead towards spire, drop down to cross bridge, bear left and cross corner of field. Cross bridge, bear right to keep in same direction with spire ahead on your left. Go through hedgerow and kiss gate and turn right across field. Cross stile by gate and then second stile on your left. Bear slightly right across field with medieval ridge and furrows still visible on the ground.

Medieval Ridge and Furrow

This was a common form of farming, particularly in the Midlands, before the enclosures of the 18th and 19th centuries. Ridges were deliberately ploughed in a clockwise spiral pattern, the soil being thrown to the right, to create a self-draining seedbed. The furrows acted as open drains and showed the boundaries between ridges. Individual famers held strips scattered in a number of open fields that surrounded each village, thus ensuring that they had sufficient land to cultivate during the normal rotation of crops over three years. Wheat and barley were planted in the first year, beans and peas in the second year and the land was then left fallow for the third year. Most ridges were 8m (11 yards) wide and 200m (220 yards or one furlong) long, the whole area being one quarter of an acre in size. Furlong is a corruption of furrow long which is the length that a team of oxen could plough without resting.

Cross stile, turn left and walk up to leave field over stile built into gate. Turn right along gravel track and follow this past houses onto road that takes you down to the main road. Cross over, turn left and walk down to the church in the centre of Louth.

Louth

It is walking round the town that makes one realise that this is a place with character. One small passage is called Paradise Smoot and another Gatherums. A notice on the town trail reads "...head down here – don't worry it is a path. It jiggles about a bit till you come across a new path. Go along it till you reach the red crossing..."

The area was settled by the Saxons, after the Romans left in AD410, and much later by the Danes. Evidence of this is in the street names ending in gate, from *gata* a Scandinavian word for street. Louth was an important market town by the time of the Doomsday Survey in 1086, one of only seven in Lincolnshire, and there were 13 watermills on the River Lud. With the development of the wool industry Louth grew in prosperity and this wealth is seen, as in so many other towns we have passed through, in the construction of an impressive church. Dedicated to St James and built in the 15th century, it has, at 295 feet (90m), the tallest parish steeple in the country. The spire was built, at a cost of £305 7s 5d, on the older tower, between 1501 and 1515. Pevsner suggests that it "has a good claim to be considered the most perfect of perpendicular steeples."

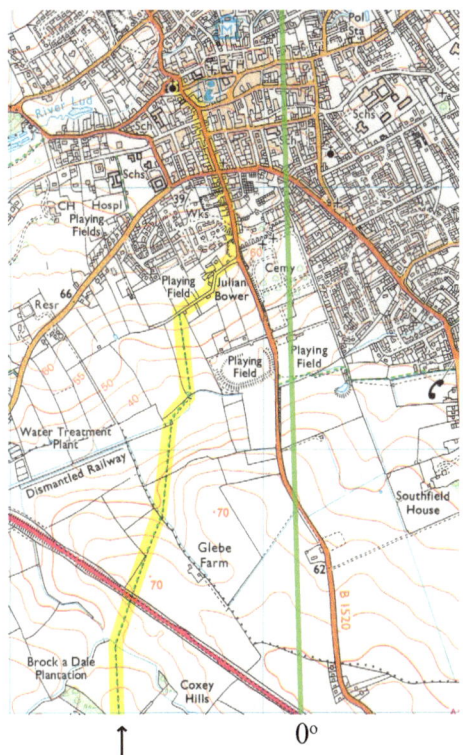

↑　　　0°

Tennyson, with his brother Charles, had his first book of poems published here in 1827 but his four years at the grammar school, from the age of seven, were not happy and thereafter Tennyson refused to walk down School House Lane whenever he visited Louth.

Today Louth is a busy and vibrant town with an active sporting and cultural scene, a cattle market (for how long?) and an industrial estate. The Art Trail includes a series of three bronze and steel figures, each discovering and contemplating the Greenwich Meridian. In *Searching*, *Mapping* and *Solution*, the figures illustrate man's attempt to understand this concept. Louth makes much of its position on the Prime Meridian with almost as many markers as East Grinstead. Try to find time to visit The Sessions House on Eastgate where you will find William Brown's panorama of the town in two large paintings. He made sketches from the church spire when scaffolding was erected to allow repairs after a lightning strike, and worked on the pictures between 1848 and 1853. They can be viewed on Wednesday and Friday mornings and at other times by telephoning 01507 355895.

We never did find the red crossing, but we did come across another sign on the town trail that reads "…Lost in Louth? Hope you discovered a place you were not looking for…". We like the playful spirit but, you will be pleased to know, we have no intention of emulating that in our guidebooks. Lost on the GMT? Never!

Facilities: Accommodation – hotels, guest houses and B&Bs; buses.

Useful Information for Boston to Louth

Tourist Information Centre
Boston   01205 356656 ticboston@boston.gov.uk

Louth   01507 601111 louthinfo@e-lindsey.gov.uk

Public Transport

		km	miles
Boston	Bus Train	0	0
Sibsey	Bus	8	5
Stickney	Bus	14.5	9
Stickford	Bus	19.5	12
Hagnaby	Bus	22	13.5
Old Bolingbroke	Bus	24	15
Hagworthingham	Bus	32	20
Somersby	Bus	37	23
Tetford	Bus	39.5	24.5
Tathwell	Bus	50	31
Louth	Bus	55	34

The services for Hagnaby, Old Bolingbroke, Bag Enderby, Somersby and Tathwell only operate if booked at least 2 hours in advance with TransLinc on 0845 234 3344.

Accommodation

Hotels and Inns	Boston, Spilsby (5 km), Louth
Guesthouses and B&B	Boston, Old Bolingbroke, West Keale (3 km), Tetford, Louth
Youth Hostel	Woody Tops at Ruckland
Campsite	Highfield Farm at Old Bolingbroke, Tetford

Tetford nestling in the Lincolnshire Wolds

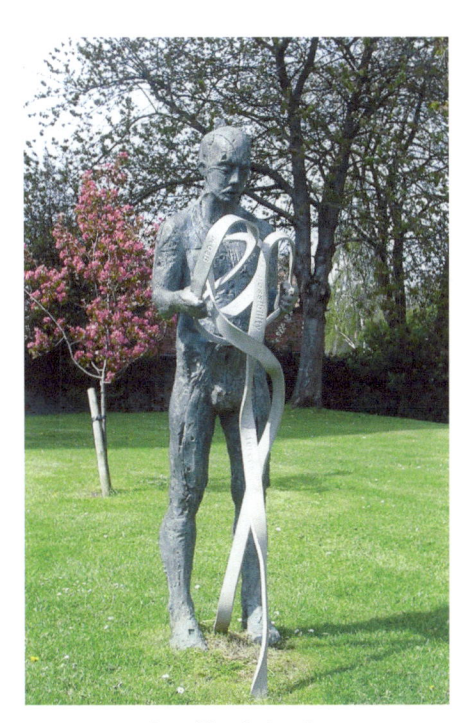

Searching in Louth

Louth to Cleethorpes

28 kilometres – 17.5 miles

A final brush with the Lincolnshire Wolds, giving fine views towards The Humber and the sea, is followed by flat fertile farmland. In medieval times this was fen and wetland, the villages are still referred to as "marsh villages", but drainage schemes begun in the 17th century and enclosures begun in the 18th century have led to the field patterns evident today. It is pleasant and easy walking and at the end is Cleethorpes, a seaside resort with all the right attributes; sea, sand, a pier and a funfair; perfect.

OS Maps:
Explorer 282: Lincolnshire Wolds North.
Explorer 283: Louth & Mablethorpe.
Once again the maps are not kind to us. Neither map gives the full route, but the missing parts are really quite small.

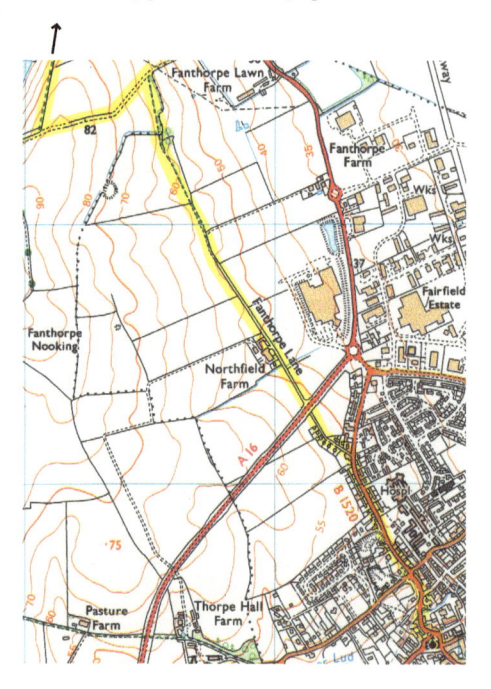

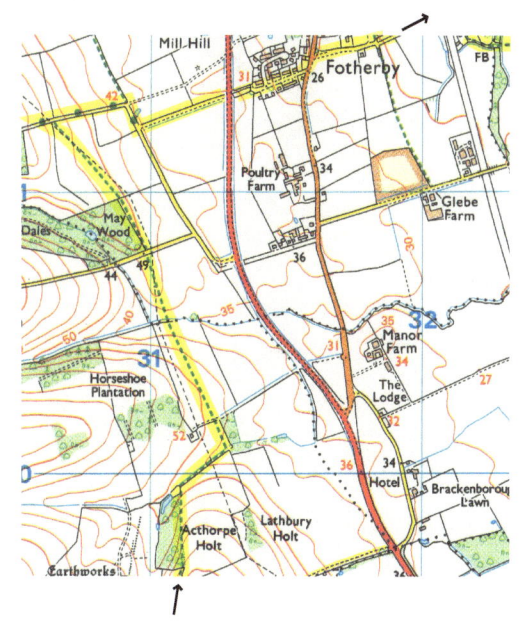

From the church, follow Bridge Street towards Grimsby, cross river and climb out of town along Grimsby Road for just under 1km. Having reached the top, as the road curves right, and 100m before a garage, turn left up Fanthorpe Lane. Follow it to the busy bypass, cross and continue ahead. Keep ahead up grassy track between hedges as road goes left into farm. Continue along edge of field with hedge on right then cross between fields with wide views opening up on your right. Go through gap, follow path ahead across field and into enclosed path with woods on your right. Keep ahead along edge of field with trees on your right and at road, turn left and walk up to the top of the hill. If you happen to have a pair of binoculars, from the layby, you can see the ships on the Humber Estuary and the lighthouse on Spurn Head in the distance ahead of you.

As the road begins to fall, turn right along path with hedge, then wood, on your left and keep on path as it drops gently down. Follow path right and at bottom, turn left over stile by gate (with waymark for Round Louth Walk). Cross field ahead, then stile and track and keep directly ahead on path across field. Cross bridge, keep ahead up rise, go through gap, cross road and follow path ahead along left edge of field. Cross bridge into next field, bear left and at road turn right. Walk down following road right, then after 100m turn left along cul-de-sac which is a bridleway that takes you to the busy A16. Cross and follow the bridleway ahead and then onto road between bungalows. At T-junction turn left, then right up Peppin Lane.

After 500m cross old railway and turn right up enclosed footpath, 30m beyond. After 300m emerge into field and follow path as it bears left towards the houses of Little Grimsby. Keep ahead along track with houses on right and at road, turn right, walk along for about 150m and turn left up bridleway by post box.

Little Grimsby
Just a little way further along the road is Little Grimsby Hall, "one of the most visually satisfying of Lincolnshire houses" according to John Harris in Pevsner's guide. It was built around 1700 for the Nelthorpe family. The church of St Edith, "near the hall and hiding in trees" is "minute (20ft long) and all whitewashed". Quite a contrast to St Botolph's in Boston.

Go through farmyard and follow grassy track ahead with wind turbines seen ahead. Cross ditch and continue on grassy path across large field, then with hedgerow on left. At road, turn left, walk along for 300m then turn right along bridleway heading for church tower and wind turbines. Cross ditch and keep ahead, mostly between hedges, for next 1km into Yarburgh.

Yarburgh
The church, dedicated to St John the Baptist, is a Grade I listed building under the care of the Churches Conservation Trust. Largely rebuilt in 1405 in the Perpendicular style after a fire, it is constructed of ironstone and chalk rubble, with limestone ashlar dressings. The beautifully detailed carvings around the west door of the tower feature Adam and Eve and the Serpent, the Lamb of God and other biblical themes. Find out about more churches to visit on the Churches Conservation Trust website listed at the back.

Facilities: post box; telephone; buses (must be booked at least 2 hours in advance on 0845 234 334).

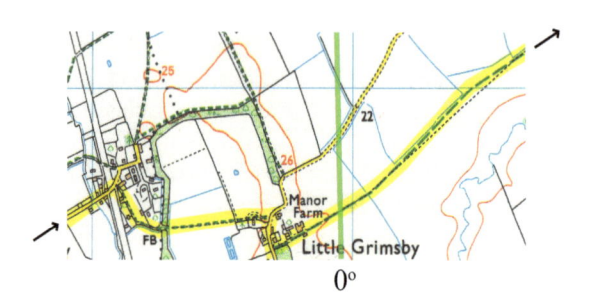

0°

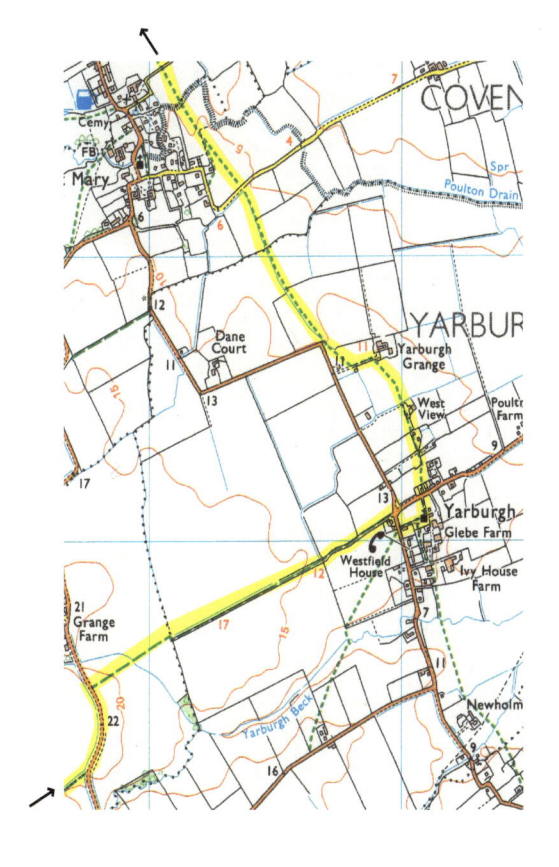

At road, turn right then, after 80m, turn left up path to church. Go past door to corner of church, turn left and follow path out to road. Turn right, then left after 20m up enclosed path. Cross stile, bear right across field, go under the branches of large tree and follow path beside fence on your left. Cross stile, second stile, driveway and keep ahead up enclosed path. Cross stile, follow path ahead around right of field, cross yet another stile and drive and bear slightly left across field. At farm drive, turn left, walk down for 100m, turn right over stile and bear left across field to stile in far left corner. Cross and follow path round to right and along edge of field, leave over stile, turn right over footbridge, then left along path, with ditch on left, for 200m. Cross bridge and stile, carry on along left edge of field, cross stile and keep ahead across field. Cross road, go through gap on bridge and follow path ahead, bearing slightly right to bridge seen ahead in middle of field. Keep ahead across next field and walk onto road.

The Covenhams
Turn left here if you are looking for refreshments at the local public house (closed on Monday). The village has two churches (though St Bartholomew's is now closed) within a few hundred yards of each other, which appears excessive. They are, of course, in separate parishes though you would find it difficult to discern from the map.

Facilities: public houses with food; buses (must be booked at least 2 hours in advance on 0845 234 3344).

Cross stile and continue ahead. Go through gap, cross field bearing left to find way out of field through hedge and over footbridge across a deep ditch. Bear left diagonally across field towards houses and at garden fences walk along to kiss gate at corner where fences meet. Go through to stile into garden, go through and at road turn right. Walk out of village for 300m and go over ladder stile on your right, joining a long distance walk with a waymark depicting a barge in full sail. Turn left and go diagonally across field following sign to Hurston's Lane. The dam wall of Covenham Reservoir (built in the 1960s to supply water to Grimsby) rises on your right. Cross ladder stile, bear left across corner of field in same direction, cross small bridge into garden and keep ahead to track. Turn right, walk up and keep ahead along edge of grass with ditch on your right. After 50m turn left, following footpath sign to Bull Bank pass bungalow on left and go directly ahead across field. At road, turn right, walk along for 200m then turn left across field. Go through gap, keep ahead across field then ditch and follow broad grassy path ahead between fields. Continue ahead onto road by farm on right and follow this (Covins Lane) for the next 300m to a T-junction.

Fulstow
Turn left here to find the discrete Meridian marker about 700m along the road. It is another one that also commemorates the Millennium. The village pub, somewhat surprisingly, also contains a shop and the village post office within its walls. After the end of WWI there was a dispute over the inclusion on a war memorial of a soldier executed for desertion. The mothers of the other soldiers killed in the war refused to have the names of their sons included unless that of the executed man was also on the memorial.

The upset within a small community like Fulstow must have been very difficult for everyone and as the matter was never resolved no memorial was erected. This omission was rectified in 2005 when a war memorial plaque was unveiled by the sister of one of the men killed in WWII at a moving ceremony where young people from the village, who were similar ages to the men and women who had died, represented them at the ceremony. There are the names of 10 men who died in WWI, including that of the man who was executed, and two women and three men who died in WWII. The women were among 26 ATS personnel killed in 1943 when a German bomb hit the hotel in Great Yarmouth where they were billeted.

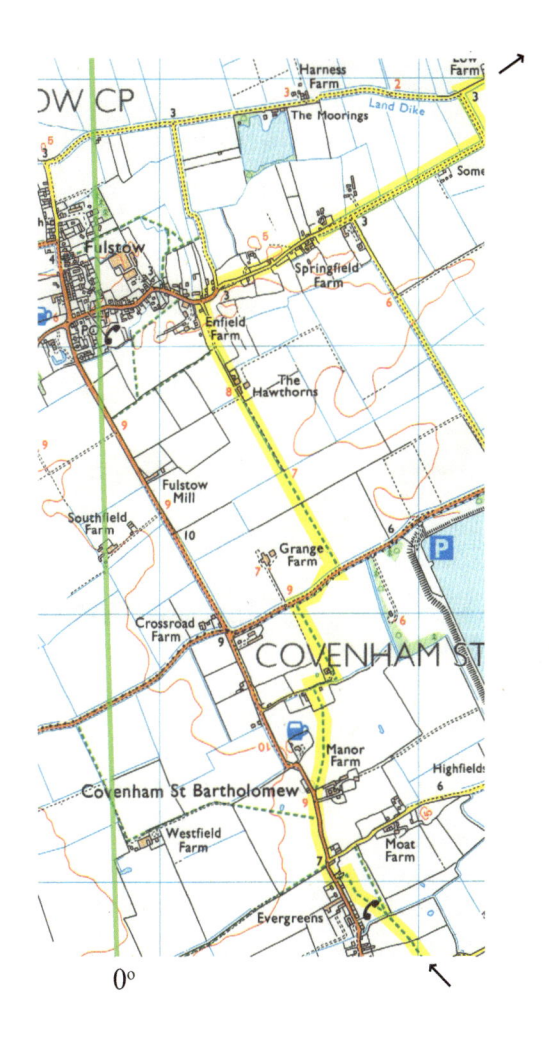

Facilities: public house with food, village store and post office; post box; telephone; buses (must be booked at least 2 hours in advance on 0845 234 3344).

Turn right, walk out of village keeping ahead at T-junction and at second junction keep ahead up Bridle Road. Follow this left and at T-junction, turn right and walk up to Fulstow Bridge.

Louth Canal
Opened in 1770, it came only a few years after England's first canal, built by the Duke of Bridgewater between Worsley and Manchester, which was completed in 1765. It is 12 miles (19km) long with eight locks which were large enough to take sea-going vessels, such as Sloops, Goole Billy-Boys and Humber Keels, so that cargoes could be transported directly to Louth without transhipment at the coast. The main exports were wool and corn and the main imports were coal, timber and groceries. Louth became a busy inland port and the area around Riverhead an industrial site with wool and grain warehouses, a ropery, a soapery, a wood yard, a tannery and fertiliser factories. The canal survived though the 19th century but difficulty with maintenance and competition from the railway led to a fall off of trade and by 1915 all trade had effectively ceased. The dramatic flood of 1920 damaged many canal structures and it was officially closed in 1924. The Louth Navigation Trust was formed in 1986 to preserve the canal and has the aim of opening it to navigation. It has an uphill struggle.

Go over bridge, turn left and walk along the canal for the next 5km to Tetney Lock, crossing the A1031 on the way. Walk up to the Crown and Anchor, follow the road left over bridge and keep on for 200m.

Tetney Lock and Tetney Marshes Nature Reserve
The lock itself has long gone; downstream is a tidal barrier and beyond that is Tetney Marshes Nature Reserve, managed by the RSPB. The reserve covers more than 3750 acres (1500 hectares) of coastal mudflats, salt marsh, dunes and saline lagoons. It supports up to 50,000 wintering and passage waders and wildfowl, around 70 pairs of breeding redshanks and many other species. The saline lagoons are populated by the rare lagoon sand shrimp, this being its northernmost site in the UK.

Facilities: public house with food; post box; telephone; buses (to Louth and must be booked at least 2 hours in advance on 0845 234 3344).

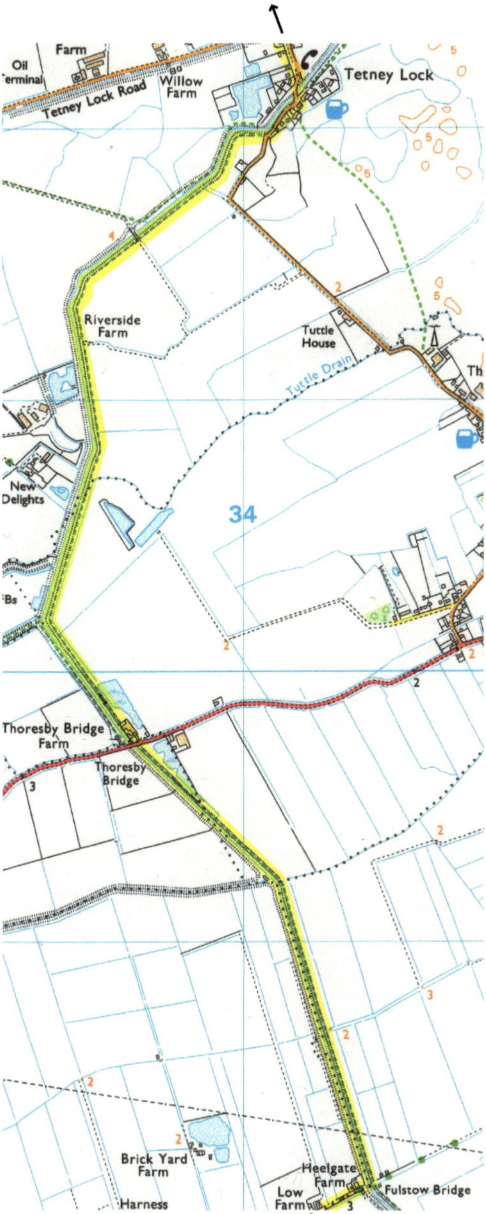

Farm
Oil
Terminal
Tetney Lock Road
Willow
Farm
Tetney Lock
Riverside
Farm
Tuttle
House
Tuttle Drain
New
Delights
34
Thoresby Bridge
Farm
Thoresby
Bridge
Brick Yard
Farm
Harness
Heelgate
Farm
Low
Farm
Fulstow Bridge

Cross drain and as road curves left, keep ahead along footpath with brick garden wall on the right. Go ahead over footbridge, through the gap and follow the path ahead along edge of field with hedge on your left. Go over second bridge, keep ahead across field to third bridge, bear left across field, go through gap with water on left and keep ahead across next field. At the fourth bridge, bear slightly left, climb up and head towards the gap in hedgerow opposite. At track, turn right and walk along with hedgerow on your left. At end, turn left by metal gates, walk up broad gravel track and after 100m turn right and follow path, with ditch and hedge on right, to sea bank ahead. Climb up for impressive views across the Humber.

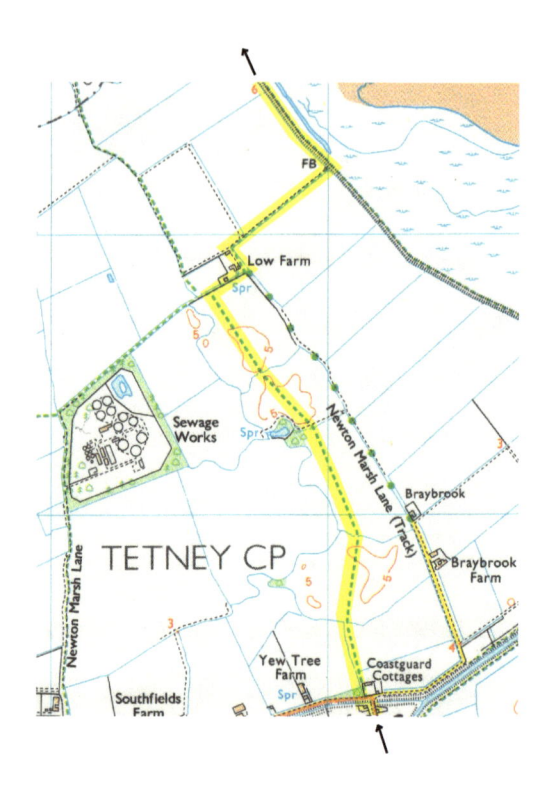

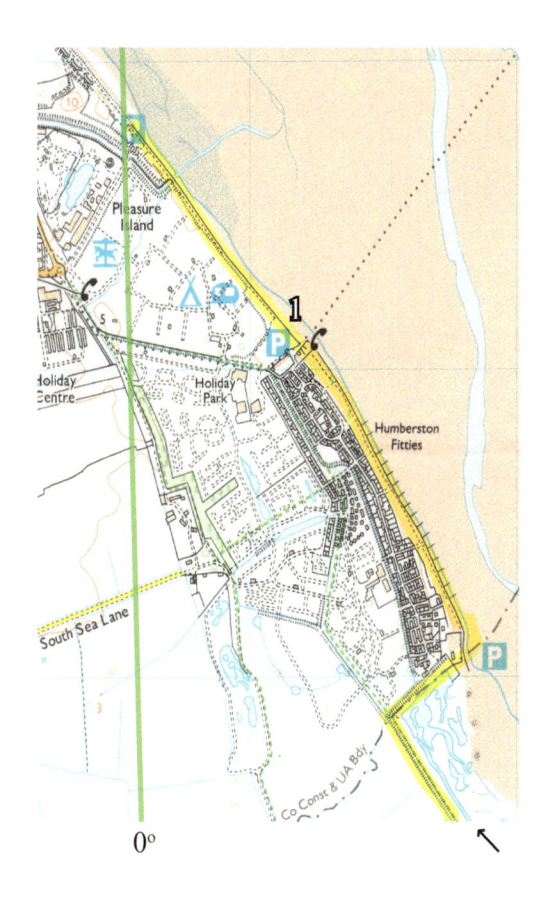

Turn left, walk past pillbox, keep on and when you reach the caravan park, turn right towards sailing club with pond on your right. Go ahead through car park onto beach and turn left. If the tide is in, or if you prefer to, you can walk along the path above the beach which you will find begins just beyond the gates into the Humber Mouth Yacht Club. Follow this path for 2km and when you reach Pleasure Island you will cross Buck Beck outfall, then pass a railway station and shortly after reach the Meridian signpost with a metal marker that crosses the path. Or, from the yacht club, you can walk along the beach for about 1km then, when you reach Anthony's Bank (1), find your way left onto the path, now with a caravan park on the left, and continue to Meridian marker. The walk starts again, on the other side of the water, at the Meridian marker just outside the village of Patrington.

Cleethorpes

A seaside resort with something for everybody; it developed after the railway arrived in 1845. You have already passed Pleasure Island Theme Park and the terminus of the Coast Light Railway and close by you will find the Jungle Zoo and the Discovery Centre. As you walk to catch the bus you will pass on the promenade Ross Castle, a folly built in 1863 by the Manchester, Sheffield and Lincoln Railway Company as a visitor attraction and named after the company's secretary, Mr Edward Ross. The same company had already constructed the promenade to prevent erosion of the seashore. The pier is considerably shorter than when first constructed. During WWII the government dismantled the middle section as part of its defence strategy for the area. After the war it could not afford to rebuild it and the isolated seaward section was demolished. Out in the estuary are two sea forts, Haile Sands Fort and Bull Fort. Constructed from massive amounts of concrete and steel during WWI, they could each accommodate a garrison of 200 men. By the time they were completed in 1917 the threat of a German invasion had receded. During WWII it would appear that they were mainly used as targets by German bombers.

Facilities: Accommodation – hotels, guest houses and B&Bs; buses; trains

Useful Information for Louth to Cleethorpes

Tourist Information Centres
Louth   01507 601111 louthinfo@e-lindsey.gov.uk
Cleethorpes   01472 323111 cleetic@nelincs.gov.uk

Public Transport

		km	miles
Louth	Bus	0	0
Fotherby	Bus	6.5	4
Covenham St Mary	Bus	13	8
Fulstow	Bus	16	10
Tetney Lock	Bus	22.5	14
Cleethorpes (Pier)	Bus, Train	31	19.5

The services for Yarburgh, Covenham St Mary, Fulstow and Tetney Lock only connect directly with Louth and only operate if booked in advance with TransLinc on 0845 234 3344.

Accommodation
Hotels and Inns   Louth, Fotherby (1.5km), Cleethorpes.
Guesthouses and B&Bs   Louth, Cleethorpes.
Campsite   Covenham St Mary, Fulstow

Louth Canal at Tetney Lock

Spurn Head and Humber Sea Forts

Royal Meridian Marker at Sunk Island

The Humber Link

Cleethorpes to Patrington by Bus or Boat

By Bus
From the Meridian marker, keep along the seafront for 3km to Cleethorpes Pier where you will find the bus stop for the Humber Flyer, bus number X1. It runs hourly to Hull from around 0700hrs to 1700hrs, except on Sundays and bank holidays, with a journey time of just under two hours. At the Paragon Interchange in Hull, catch bus number 76 or 77 which leaves half-hourly and takes an hour to Patrington. In the centre of Patrington, bear right into Market Place, continue along into High Street and follow it past the church into Eastgate. Turn right into Welwick Road, walk between flats and bungalows and keep on as the road curves left by a children's play area. About 100m after the riding stables you will find the Meridian marker.

By Boat
A number of local sailors have indicated that they would be prepared to ferry walkers across the Humber Estuary to Spurn Head. This is a lot more complicated than it sounds but well worth the effort. Go to the website for the latest information.

From the beach at Spurn Point, find your way onto the Spurn Footpath, which is more interesting than simply walking up the road. When it petered out we chose to walk up the beach to the Visitors Centre and then along the road to Kilnsea. At The Crown and Anchor public house, climb onto the defensive bank with the Humber Estuary on your left and stay on it for the next 9.5km. At Welwick Bank, keep ahead along the track towards Patrington Haven for just over 2km, passing through nature reserves and round lakes. This is not marked as a public right of way but is well used by bird watchers, dog owners and horse riders. Turning right up Saltmarsh Lane takes you to the main road where you turn right for the Meridian marker.

The Humber Link and Royal Marker Diversion

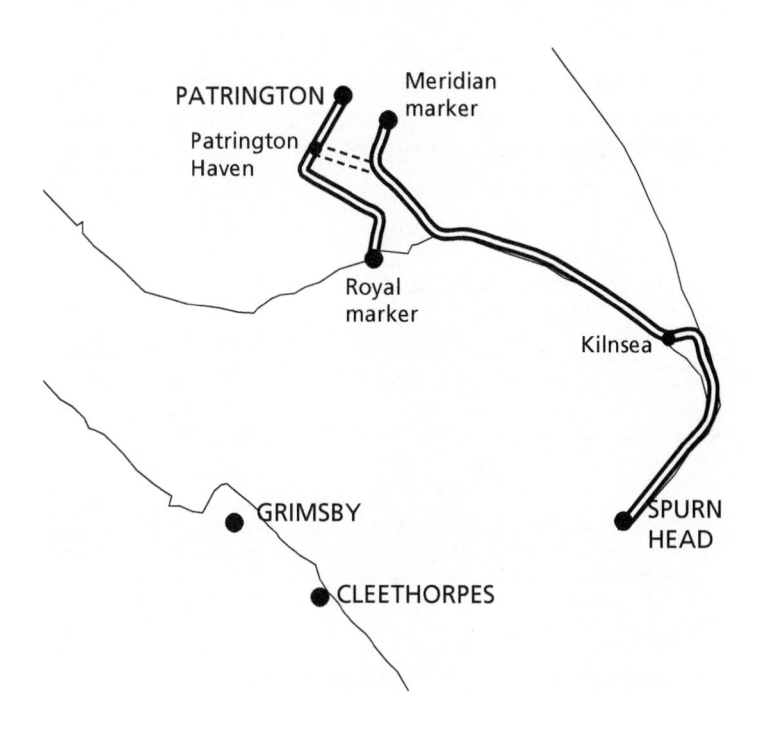

The Royal Meridian Marker

Strictly speaking the walk should restart on the north bank of the estuary at Sunk Island. There is a 5 foot (1.5m) high stone triangular obelisk, with a crown on the front of the base, placed on the Greenwich Meridian by the Crown Estate Commissioners. It commemorates the raising of the outer banks of the Humber Estuary, between 1983 and 1985, to 3.3m above mean high water. Getting there is easy. Unfortunately the only way back to Patrington is to retrace your steps. Rightly or wrongly, we have decided to allow you the choice as to whether or not you complete this short diversion. Go through Patrington Haven and then follow the road beside Winestead Drain to the coast where you should turn right along the inner embankment, because the outer one has been deliberately breached to create a new salt water habitat. The distance is just short of 4 miles (6km). Returning to the start of the next section, you may, if you wish, turn right along the footpath at Holmwood Farm in Patrington Haven and then left up Saltmarsh Lane.

Patrington to Sand le Mere

15 kilometres – 9.5 miles

This is a continuation of the landscape south of the Humber, fertile farmland criss-crossed with drainage ditches. It is just about as gentle as walking can be, which allows you to wind down as you come to the end of the trail.

OS Map:
Explorer 292: Withernsea & Spurn Head.

Patrington
Full, as it is, of useful shops and places to stay and eat, you will, nevertheless, remember Patrington for its church, dedicated to St Patrick. Pevsner puts it this way: "For sheer architectural beauty few parish churches in England can vie with Patrington." and "The spire of Patrington is one of the finest in the country, not at all showy, but wonderfully satisfying in the way it rises from behind an octagonal screen of Perpendicular panels, two to each side." Praise indeed. The top of the spire was dangerously cracked by a 5.3 magnitude earthquake, centred about 23 miles (37km) away at Market Rasen in February 2008. The top was stabilised with temporary long stainless-steel straps before a permanent repair was affected. In the 18th century Patrington Haven was a busy little port, but the construction of defensive banks and land reclamation moved the coast away from Patrington and led to the silting up of the harbour.

Facilities: Accommodation – B&Bs; public houses with food; buses.

From the Meridian marker walk (back) up the road into Patrington following it right between flats and bungalows and turn right down Holmpton Road. Follow this for just over 2km passing on the way a construction of a pair of whalebones set into small brick plinths. Its purpose is not given, but it is a reminder of this area's connection with the whaling industry, more of which anon. About 600m after passing the double fronted farmhouse set back from the road, turn left along bridleway with ditch on your right. Follow ditch as it bears right and at corner of field keep ahead, cross ditch and follow straight grassy track for the next 1km. At field corner follow track left between hedgerows and walk out to the road. Turn right walk along 400m and just after 30 speed limit sign, as road goes right, keep ahead up side road and follow this for 300m to the church.

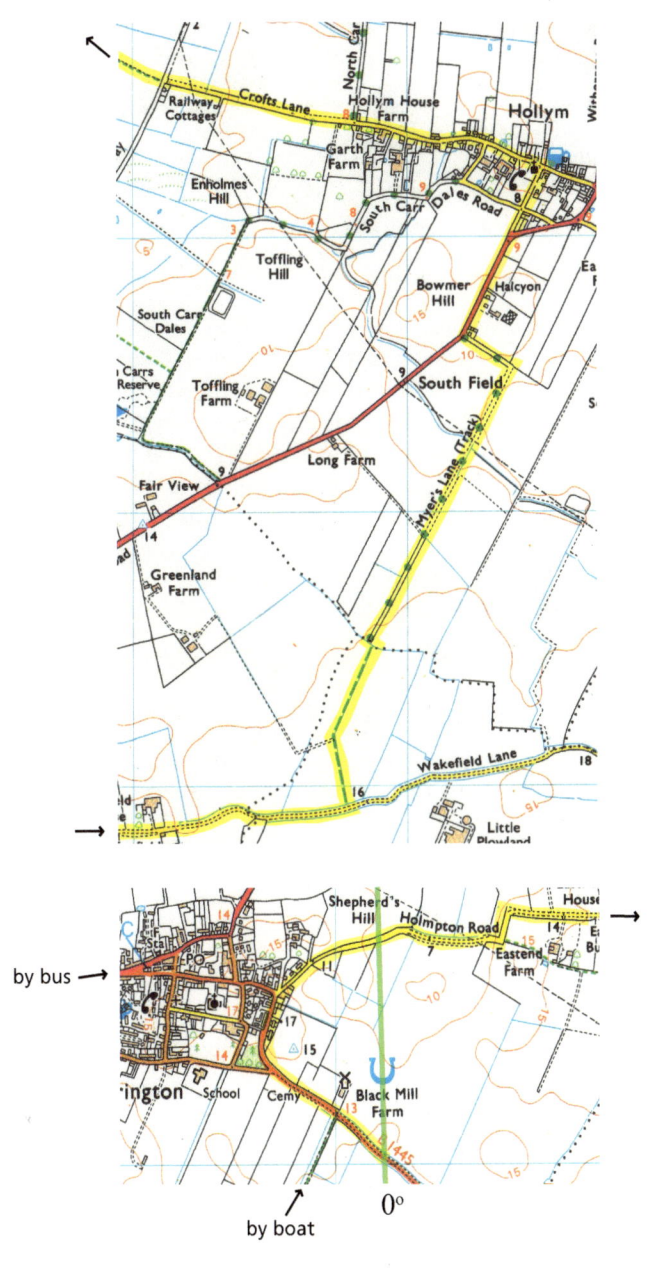

Turn left and walk up the road for 1.5km with views of the sea and the lighthouse at Withernsea on your right. Cross the old railway track and follow the path as it bears slightly right across field, heading for the solitary brown house ahead.

43

Hollym

The Plough Inn is a 16th century coaching inn constructed of wattle and daub, one of few such buildings left in the area. Another rare construction is The Pinfold, a circular area surrounded by a cobble wall dating from the 18th century. Stray animals were kept in the fold until their owners retrieved them for a fee of six (old) pennies. George Hunter, the village cobbler, was the last known 'pinder'. Turn right to find it after 200m.

Facilities: public house with food and accommodation; buses.

Cross bridge and stile (the last one on the GMT), keep ahead on the same line, and go into next field bearing left. through two small gates. Keep ahead towards farm building and go through farm gate(s) onto track between fences and then with ditch and hedge on your right. At the end of track turn right onto road and walk up past farm on your left. Keep on this road for 1.5km and at T-junction turn right onto quite a busy road towards Withernsea. After 200m turn left onto road to Rimswell (200m further on towards Withernsea there is another large white sign marking the Meridian) and walk into village.

Rimswell

Rimswell is in the parish of Owthorne (now part of Withernsea) and the church of St Mary was built in 1801 to replace the old church at Owthorne which finally fell into the sea in 1816. As it is over a mile (2km) inland it should be safe from the sea for the moment. The Rimswell Water Tower was built in 1916 by Hull Corporation Waterworks. The two water tanks hold 400,000 gallons (nearly 2 million litres), sufficient in those days to last South Holderness for two days.

Holderness and Spurn Head

One hundred thousand years ago the area now called Holderness was under the sea. The shoreline ran along the eastern edge of the Yorkshire Wolds. During the Ice Ages vast quantities of soil and stones were pushed south by the ice and deposited here, as boulder clay, when the ice retreated. Boulder clay is soft and easily eroded by the sea. Over the course of thousands of years Spurn Head formed from the sand washed down the coast from the north by a process called long shore drift. As the coastline was washed away and retreated to the west Spurn Head also moved west. This natural process was arrested about 150 years ago by the erection of coastal barriers which stopped Spurn Head's drift to the west with consequences too complicated to go into here. Sooner or later something will have to be done in order to allow Spurn Head to move again but nobody has worked out what.

0°

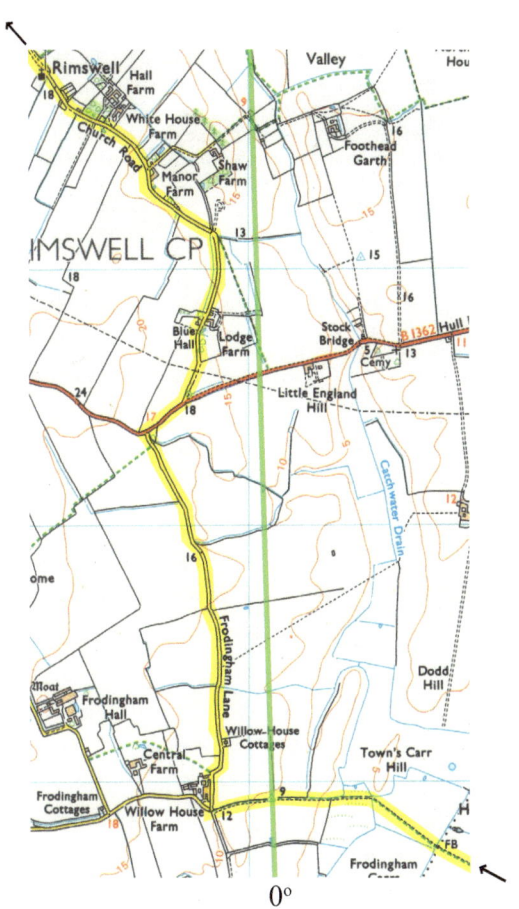

Old Bones

45

This part of Holderness has a connection back to Old Bolingbroke. It is here in 1399 that Henry Bolingbroke returned from exile to challenge Richard II landing at the village of Ravenspur, somewhere east of Easington and long lost to the sea. His powerbase was in the north and he quickly gained the support of powerful barons that ultimately led to Richard's defeat. Whaling ships were sailing from Hull in the 16th century but it was in the middle of the 18th century that the whaling industry in Hull began to grow, to the point that at the start of the 19th century Hull vessels made up 40% of the British whaling fleet. Whaling was a dangerous business with many ships crushed in the Arctic ice. Investors withdrew their money and the industry in Hull declined, the last boat sailing out of Hull was wrecked off the Lincolnshire coast in 1869.

Spurn Head and the flat sands of the Humber Estuary are a mecca for bird watchers. During the autumn migration tens of thousands of birds stop over to feed whilst on their journeys from Greenland and Northern Europe to Southern Europe and Africa. At the tip of Spurn Head are the lifeboat, stationed here for quick access to the sea, and the pilot boats. Twenty five thousand ships a year require the services of the Humber Pilots, very nearly 70 a day. The terminal at Easington is where natural gas is brought directly into the UK from the Norwegian Sleipner gas field along the Langeled pipeline, which is the world's longest undersea pipeline. At RAF Holmpton you can visit a massive underground concrete bunker which was completed in 1953 and formed part of the early warning radar system during the Cold War.

After passing the church turn right towards Tunstall and Roos. Follow this road for about 1.5km and at main road cross left onto path along edge of field with a stream on your left. Keep along this path beside Tunstall Drain which is often quite overgrown. Make sure that you keep to the stream-side of any fences that you encounter. (New flood defence embankments will be constructed at some time which will completely disrupt this part of the walk. Follow the diversions and please let us know how you manage) Scramble up the sea bank, turn left and walk for about 100m to where the Meridian crosses at latitude 53 degrees 4558 min N. This is the end of the Greenwich Meridian Trail.

Getting from the finish

Walking the 4.5km (3 miles) to Withernsea is best along the beach, tide permitting. The cliff-top path is easily passable but perilously close to the edge in places and is not marked as a public right of way, though clearly well used. Alternatively, find your way back to Withernsea Road (B1242) and catch the bus to Withernsea that runs two-hourly until about 1430 hours. From Withernsea buses run to Hull every half hour in the morning and hourly in the afternoon, with a journey time of a little over one hour. If you have not already visited Spurn Head, we encourage you to spend a day there before your journey home. It is rather special and should not be missed while you are in the area.

0°

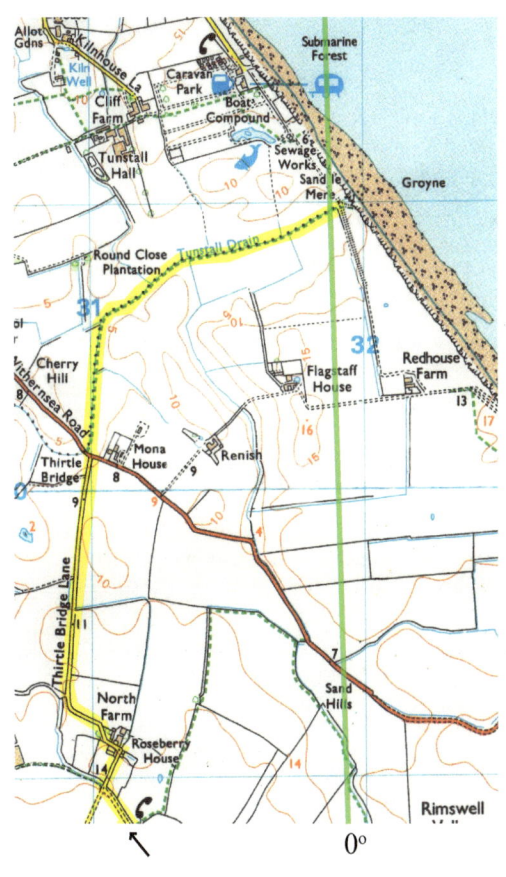

Beach at Sand le Mere The End of the GMT

47

Sand le Mere

The name, Sand le Mere, is derived from Sandley mere, a lake that once, hundreds of years ago, emptied into Tunstall Drain. The drain flows westward, joins with Keyingham Drain and eventually runs out into the Humber at Stone Creek. Erosion by the sea reduced the mere to a depression in the cliffs and a protective bank had been built as early as 1622. As you can see the present embankment is being rapidly attacked by the sea and there is a real risk of damaging flooding should a breach occur. East Yorkshire County Council and the Environment Agency are committed to a scheme to build a new defensive embankment 750m inland, but funding and engineering issues have delayed the start of the project. Once the new defences are in place the present embankment will not be maintained and will eventually be breached with uncertain results. The authorities believe that sand dunes will almost certainly form over time, possibly sealing the breach. These changes will definitely move the point where it will be sensible to end the trail but not in a predictable way. Keep up with developments, as they occur, on our website.

The pillbox, probably a type 24, you can see north of Tunstall Drain is one of three in this area. They represent all that remains intact of an extensive set of defensive structures built in 1940 and early 1941 when the threat of a German invasion was at its greatest. The embankment across the drain was only built, by the army, after the war so the gap in the cliffs at this point would have been vulnerable to a German landing force. Along this stretch of coast were gun and light emplacements, anti-tank blocks and ditches, fire trenches and defence posts. These are all now lost to the sea. You can find a full description by Austin J. Ruddy on the Pillbox Study Group website. His damning assessment is that these defences would have done little to delay a determined attack. There are many big chunks of concrete strewn along the beach but how much comes from the WWII defences and how much from other structures and efforts to prevent erosion by the sea is hard to discern

Withernsea

Withernsea is a busy holiday town with lots going on all year round, especially at the Meridian Centre. The town's most famous landmark is the lighthouse, completed in 1894 and in use until 1976, sited several hundred metres from the shore, one of only a handful of inland lighthouses. You can climb the 144 steps for views as far as the Humber Bridge on a clear day and also visit the museum to find out more about the town and about Kay Kendall who was born just a few yards away. Interestingly odd is the castellated construction, said to be modelled on the gateway to Conway Castle, on the seafront. It is the entrance to the pier, except the pier is no longer there. Completed in 1877, the pier was 1196 feet (368m) long and for two years was deemed to be a success with large numbers of day trippers from Hull being charged one (old) penny for admission. Unfortunately, ships kept crashing into the pier gradually reducing its length until in 1893 it was reduced to just 50 feet by a particularly spectacular collapse caused by the timber cargo of the steel barque Henry Parr which broke in two in a gale.

The piles of the pier were demolished one by one with a "fearful noise and a brilliant display of sparks." The remnants were finally removed in 1903 when the seawall and promenade were constructed. For the full story see the information plaques on the sculpture/bench, called Pier Piece, on the promenade.

Facilities: Accommodation – hotel, campsites; public houses with food; buses

Useful Information for Patrington to Sand le Mere

Public Transport

		km	miles
Patrington	Bus	0	0
Hollym	Bus	5.5	3.5

Accommodation
Hotels and Inns: Hollym, Withernsea
Guesthouses and B&Bs: Patrington
Campsites   Withernsea, Sand le Mere

The Greenwich Meridian

In 1884, US President Chester A. Arthur convened the International Meridian Conference in order to decide upon a Prime Meridian. Delegates from 25 countries attended and after weeks of debates it was agreed that the Royal Observatory at Greenwich should be adopted as Zero Degrees Longitude for all countries. The importance of this is two-fold. Firstly, it ensures that all charts and maps use the same latitude and longitude readings for fixing positions. It turned out that nearly three quarters of charts already used Greenwich as Zero Meridian thus agreeing on Greenwich was the least disruptive choice. The other aspect was the creation of Greenwich Mean Time (GMT) and the 'universal day'. The 'universal day' starts at midnight at Greenwich and is the same all over the world. All countries derive their time from GMT, except that technically it is not GMT anymore, it is Coordinated Universal Time. Astronomical measurements and atomic clock readings from around the world are coordinated at the International Time Bureau in Paris. So when you hear the time signal on your radio at breakfast time, just remember that they are French pips that you are listening to.

Bibliography

The Buildings of England: Lincolnshire by Nikolaus Pevsner and John Harris. Published by Penguin Books, 1964.

History and Guide to The Maud Foster Mill. Compilation and Design by Luke Bonwick.

The Oxford History of England The Fifteenth Century 1399 – 1485 by E F Jacob. Published by Oxford University Press, 1961. Reprinted 1997.

A History of Britain: At the Edge of the World? 3000 BC – AD 1603 by Simon Sharma. Published by BBC Worldwide Ltd, 2000.

Historical Atlas of Britain. General Editors: Malcom Falkus and John Gillingham. Published by Book Club Associates, 1981.

The Royal Village of Old Bolingbroke. A Short Guide of the Castle and Church. Published by the Churchwardens and Parochial Church Council, 2003.

Hagworthingham. Notes on Holy Trinity Church by D L Brown. 2011. Copy supplied by Sue Archibald, Clerk to Hagworthingham Parish Council.

The Tennyson Family & Their Villages by John Large. Self published, 1999. ISBN 9780955084218

The South Wolds. In Tennyson's Time and Today by John Large. Self published, 2011.
ISBN 978-0-9564302-4-3

Official Louth Town Guide 2011 – 2012. Published by Plus Publishing Services.

The Buildings of England Yorkshire: York & The East Riding by Nikolaus Pevsner. Published by Penguin Books, 1972.

Web bibliography

		Confirmed on
Introduction and Boston	*Foxe's Book of Martyrs* on *In Our Time*. Broadcast on 18-11-10 with Melvyn Bragg, Diarmaid MacCulloch, Justin Champion and Elizabeth Evenden. Available as a podcast on the BBC website.	12-02-12
	The Unabridged Acts and Monuments Online or TAMO (HRI Online Publications, Sheffield, 2011) at http://www.johnfoxe.org	13-02-12

	The Acts and Monuments – Wikipedia, the free Encyclopedia at http://en.wikipedia.org/wiki/Foxe%27s_Book_of_Martyrs	13-02-12
	Welcome to Boston (vistoruk.com) at http://www.bostonuk.com/	03-03-12
	A Brief History of Boston, Lincolnshire, England by Tim Lambert at http://www.localhistories.org/boston.html (These are two excellent websites.)	03-03-12
Stickney and Paul Verlaine	Stickney History – The History of a Lincolnshire Village by Martin Gosling at http://stickneyhistory.co.uk/	30-08-12
	Paul Verlaine at http://en.wikipedia.org/wiki/Paul_Verlaine	30-08-12
Lincolnshire Aviation Heritage Centre	The only place in the UK where you can ride a Lancaster Bomber at http://www.lincsaviation.co.uk	22-06-12
Old Bolingbroke	Bolingbroke Castle at http://community.lincolnshire.gov.uk/BolingbrokeCastle/index.asp?catId=21787	03-10-12
Richard II	Richard II of England in Wikipedia at http://en.wikipedia.org/wiki/Richard_II_of_England	23-06-12
Battle of Winceby	Civil War in Lincolnshire at http://www.british-civil-war.co.uk/military/1643-lincolnshire.htm	18-07-12
	UK Battlefield Resource Centre at http://www.battlefieldtrust.com/resource-centre/civil-war/battleview.asp?BattleFieldId=48	18-07-12
Snipe Dales	Snipe Dales Country Park and Nature Reserve at http://www.lincstrust.org.uk/reserve/snipe/description.php	03-10-12
Hagworthingham	Hagworthingham Parish Council at http://parishes.lincolnshire.gov.uk/Hagworthingham/section.asp?catId=28966	23-06-12
Tetford	Tetford Longhorn Herd at http://www.tetfordlonghorns.co.uk/index.html	23-06-12
Tathwell	The Parish of St Vedast alias Foster at http://www.vedast.org.uk/history.html	23-06-12
Medieval Ridge and Furrow	Medieval fields in their many forms by David Hall at http://www.britarch.ac.uk/ba/ba33/ba33/ba33feat.html#hall	23-06-12
Louth	Louth Historic Capital of the Lincolnshire Wolds at http://www.louth.org/index.htm	23-06-12

Yarburgh	St John the Baptist Church, Yarburgh at http://en.wikipedia.org/wiki.St_John_the_Baptist%27s_Church._Yarburgh	18-07-12
	The Churches Conservation Trust at http://www.visitchurches.org.uk/Ourchurches/Completelistofchurches/Church-of-St-John-the-Baptist	18-07-12
The Covenhams	Village website at http://www.covenham.org.uk/index.htm	18-07-12
Fulstow	Village website at http://fulstow.net	18-07-12
	WW2 Casualties of Fulstow Lincolnshire at http://2ndww.blogspot.co.uk/2010/11/ww2-casualties-of-fulstow-lincolnshire.html	18-07-12
Louth Canal	Peter Hardcastle. The Original - Canals & Waterways: Roots & Routes at http://www.canals.btinternet.co.uk/canals/louth.htm	19-07-12
	Louth Navigation Trust at http://www.louthcanal.org.uk/index.html	19-07-12
Tetney Marshes Nature Reserve	The RSPB: Tetney Marshes at http://rspb.org.uk/reserves/guide/t/tetneymarshes/index.aspx	28-08-12
Cleethorpes	Welcome to Cleethorpes visitoruk.com at http://cleethorpesuk.com/historic_site.php?f=Cleethorpes	28-08-12
Hollym	The Village at http://www.hollym.org.uk/index.htm	28-08-12
Rimswell	Welcome to Hornsea visitoruk.com at http://www.visitoruk.com/historydetail.php?id=26519&f=hornsea	28-08-12
Sand le Mere	Tunstall A History of the County of York East Riding: Volume 7 (pp. 172-181) at http://www.british-history.ac.uk/report.aspx?compid=16144	31-07-12
	Sand-le-Mere Defence of a Coastal Inlet. Pillbox Study Group at http://www.pillbox-study-group.org.uk/sandlemerepage.htm	31-07-12

Lightning Source UK Ltd.
Milton Keynes UK
UKHW051528300519
343570UK00001B/1/P